Enete Enterprises, LLC

6504 N Omaha Ave
Oklahoma City, OK 73116 (USA)

1st publication of
Becoming an Expat: Thailand

** *Becoming an Expat guidebook series* **

Gibbs, Laura & Enete, Shannon 2014

Becoming an Expat Thailand: your guide to moving abroad / Laura Gibbs, Shannon Enete

ISBN-13: 978-1938216084
ISBN-10: 1938216083

Registered with the Library of congress: 1-1803572121

Printed in the United States of America
www.EneteEnterprises.com

OTHER BOOKS BY

BECOMING AN EXPAT

Becoming an Expat:
Costa Rica

Becoming an Expat:
Ecuador

Becoming an Expat
COOKBOOK: Costa Rica

UPCOMING BOOKS

Becoming a Nomad
Becoming an Expat: Brazil
Becoming an Expat: Mexico
2015: Panama, Belize editions

VISIT: BecominganExpat.com

To see updates in-between editions, find additional resources, and discover what's coming up next!

DEDICATION

I would like to say a big thank you to everyone I interviewed. Your experiences, advice, knowledge, and patience helped me create an extraordinary expat guidebook. I'd like to mention Kayla Colyard, Jason Berkley, Sandy Dhaliwal, Alex Gunn, Rosanne Turner, Aaron Johnson, Melanie Long, Justine Bristow, Chris Taylor, Johan Pellsater, Nicolas, Vicky, Dillon the dog, and Henry for answering my countless questions about visas and logistics. I'd also like to thank Lee whose comments always guided me in the right direction and Shannon Enete who made this book happen and for her kind feedback.

I'd like to thank my parents who supplied coffee and a floor to sleep on during a portion of this book project. Finally, I dedicate this book to those considering a move to Thailand - this book was written for you - I hope you enjoy your journey!

TABLE OF CONTENTS

THE BASICS

BASICS

Thailand has an impressive expatriate community. People from all walks of life end up here for a variety of reasons: high quality of life, low cost of living, good weather, beautiful beaches, ease of domestic travel, decent flight connections, friendly people, and you can't forget the excellent food!

Ten years ago the expat community was almost exclusively retirees. Many of these golden-year globe-trotters were men looking for a country that wouldn't judge them if they started drinking at 1pm and dated a woman half their age. Over the last decade, the composition of the expat community has drastically transformed. Thailand is an increasingly attractive place for the younger generations who seek a taste of independence, volunteerism, language exposure to hone their teaching skills, and to reshape their perceptions of the world and how to live in it.

Entrepreneurs, writers, and *digital nomads* come to work, write, and develop business ideas without the associated costs of failure. Families can set themselves up in comfy houses with gardens, tucked away in safe neighborhoods, all while sending their children to good international schools at a fraction of the cost of a life in North America. Retirees can live comfortably on their pensions and enjoy an active community. Still others choose to live in Thailand part-time, thus avoiding the hot and rainy season and balancing a life with loved ones in their home country.

HISTORY

Thai history is a history of Kingdoms. Thailand's borders were ever changing due to the rising and falling of empire after empire. The Kingdoms of Lanna (in the north) and Sukhothai (central) rose and reclaimed areas taken by the Khmer empire, only then to be invaded by the Ayutthaya Kingdom whose citizens reportedly called themselves Tai (ah, recognize that name eh?). The earliest known Thais were agriculturists. They came from modern day India and Myanmar and brought Buddhism with them.

The Ayutthaya period is known as a time where European merchants and traders frequented the country, amazed at the expanse and glory of the kingdom. This growth did not last long, because the neighboring Burmese grew in power and after repeated invasion attempts, managed to topple and occupy central Thailand. The Burmese destroyed most of Ayutthaya's temples in the process (the remains are now a UNESCO heritage site).

In an attempt to avoid Burmese control, much of the kingdom relocated south and established modern day Siam. Thus marked the beginning of a country ruled by kings, from Rama I to present day King Bumibol Adulyadej, Rama IX.

The leadership and actions of the past kings has helped mold the Thailand we see today. Through diplomatic relations with European countries over the years, Thailand is one of the few South East Asian countries that was never colonized by foreign powers. Instead, it benefited from trade and capitalized on the ideas that foreigners brought, including an array of topics ranging from schools and democracy to post offices, roads, and railways.

The monarchy has brought forward great advancements, because of this, the people have remained strongly devoted to the system in place which isn't something other Asian countries can say. Kings are so highly admired, there's even a law carrying a prison sentence forbidding the utterance of negative comments about any Thai king alive or dead.

CULTURE

Thailand has a deep and drastically different culture than the Western world. No matter how good your Thai is or how long you live here, to fully grasp and be accepted into the colorful Thai culture proves unattainable for the non-native. To them, you represent a high earning power. Once you accept their view of you, you'll understand Thais and their actions a whole lot better.

Despite being the perpetual outsider, Thais are very welcoming, open, and friendly to everyone; and boy are they curious. Expect countless questions about yourself, age, and weight! Don't be offended, in Thailand it's common to speak about these things. They might also call you fat, but again, don't take it personally. It's cute to be a bit chubby in their culture, it shows you enjoy food.

For such a thin nation, Thais are crazy about eating. It's okay to eat at any time of day. They snack between snacks! Knowing this might help explain the endless street stalls and 7-elevens across the country. Besides pleasure and sustenance, eating is a communal experience in Thailand. Every counter and table in Thailand is "family-style eating." They will offer you their food and expect to try some of yours!

Much of Thailand is represented with the "family-style" meal, a laid back approach to sharing life. If you're happy then they're happy. As long as everyone is happy, *mai pen rai* (then it doesn't matter). However, there are a few instances in which rules should be strictly adhered to. They include: references to Buddhism, the King, and respect. If you're courteous and respectful, it's unlikely you'll encounter any problems. If you're rude to people or assume Thais are beneath you, then you might want to watch your back.

TOURISM

Thailand is a great place for tourists, everyone speaks a little English, the country has stunning sights, and compared to neighboring countries, it's super cheap! It's no wonder that in 2012, Thailand received 22.3 million visitors (Tourism Authority of Thailand).[1] Not only is Thailand home to stunning beaches (with beach weather year-round), a rich culture, great shopping, and cheap 5 star hotels, Bangkok's international airport, Suvarnabhumi, is a South East Asian air hub! That means you can easily fly to almost any major Asian, European, and Middle East city from Bangkok. Additionally, there are low cost direct flights to China since there are more Chinese in Thailand than any other ethnicity. A steady stream of Europeans and Russians has resulted in niche tour guides, restaurants, and hotels catering to almost every major nationality and language.

POLITICS

I won't bore you with the history of Thai politics, it's complex and mostly irrelevant to expats. There are only two figures you really need to take note of: Taksin Shinawatra and his sister Yingluck Shinawatra. Taksin, a former police colonel turned politician, became prime minister in 2001. He was originally known for initiating numerous reforms that benefited impoverished citizens. Shortly after his re-election in 2005, the public got wind of some private investments that benefited the Shinawatra family. Taksins success and reputation began to unravel. What may have been considered "normal business in politics" in thousands of corrupt countries around the world was not tolerated in Thailand. A coup in 2006 left Taksin in a self-imposed exile in Dubai.

---

[1] website: http://www.tourismthailand.org/

Five years later, Taksin's little sister, Yingluck, entered the scene with a relatively new party, Pheu Thai. Surprisingly, despite the controversial family connection, she won the election and became Prime Minister. Her campaign, promising price guarantees and gains for the rural poor, secured her seat. However, the educated middle class feared she was just a puppet for her brother. After attempting to pass an Amnesty bill in late 2013 that would allow Taksin to return without prosecution, the public erupted. Riots and protests quickly sent her running from her office.

The Shinawatra family drama is the latest saga in a country prone to coups and protests. Despite this, Thailand remains quite stable with the majority of the government under Royal, rather than party control. The fluctuations of Thai politics haven't heavily affected expatriates.

EXPAT EXPERIENCE

Regarding the 2013 protests:

"Here, in Chiang Mai, I didn't notice any major disruptions. Once or twice there were political events at the gates and around the moat. I did notice the police presence was reduced in Chiang Mai during the protests, most likely because they were redirected to the BKK to help out. To tell you the truth, I was happy to see them go. Things run a lot smoother around here without the police! Whenever an expat starts getting worked up about Thai politics, I can't help but have a bit of a chuckle. If this were my home country, I would be beyond upset with the way it is being run. Corruption, lies, and nepotism are the rule here rather than the exception. Thailand is a lovely country, but it's being run into the ground by incompetent leadership."

~ Jason, International School Teacher

STABILITY

Despite all the political issues over the last decade, Thailand adamantly separates the tourism sector from any political disturbances. Throughout the political protests of 2010 and 2013, and the floods of 2011, life outside the affected areas of Bangkok continued as usual. Expatriates are not targets and are considered safe during major events, but are advised to avoid protest areas as a precaution. In most cases, Thais will take care and steer foreigners away from trouble, regardless if you're a tourist or expat. In return, they expect you not to get involved. The general consensus is that Thailand's politics are Thailand's business, and as you may recall from the culture section, living in Thailand does not make you Thai.

Not only do Thais work together for tourism efforts, they lend a helping hand whenever they see the need. The 2004 Tsunami brought the entire country together to assist the victims without discrimination. Even though the tourism sector was badly affected for years, this disaster is a prime example of how Thailand can bounce back.

Only the 'Deep South' could be classified as *deeply* unstable due to continuous fighting for the provinces to gain autonomy and loosen their ties to Bangkok. Travel in the southernmost provinces is not advised and most foreigners oblige.

For safety advice, check your embassy's travel advisory website
✦British foreign-travel-advice website.[2]
✦US Travel advisory site[3]
✦Canada's Travel Advisory[4] site

---

[2] https://www.gov.uk/foreign-travel-advice/thailand/safety-and-security

[3] http://bangkok.usembassy.gov/service.html

[4] http://travel.gc.ca/destinations/thailand

ECONOMY

Most tourists who visit Thailand could argue that tourism has to be the biggest economic sector. No matter where you look, it's in your face. However, you would be making an *ass*—umption. Thailand's economy is actually fueled by exports, particularly rice. Agriculture and manufacturing are the backbone of this robust SE Asia economy. Only Singapore and Malaysia have more purchasing power in the region.

Even though tourism doesn't top the budget, it's an important aspect of the country's economy. Particularly because it provides many poor citizens a cash-flow and entrepreneurial opportunities. The export and manufacturing industries have a long history of monopolization by wealthy families, corrupt politicians, and conglomerates (*the Shinawatra family come to mind*). While the tourism industry isn't heavily effected by the on-again off-again political scuffles, other sectors can take heavy hits. Take for example the drop in rice exports and investment after the 2013 riots demanding Yingluck to step down.

Owning a business in Thailand isn't for the weak of spirit. Many expat business owners will tell you with the right business and perseverance, it can succeed. We'll discuss further in the **Work Hard Play Hard** section.

CRIME

Thailand is a relatively safe country. The most common cause for concern is petty theft. Tourists and expats are often viewed as wealthy, and easy targets for pickpocketing, bag snatching, and small scams. Most thefts are after cash, passports, i-devices, or other electronics of high value (*which can often be re-bought on Khao San Road in Bangkok*). Violent assaults or attacks against expats are rare and are usually the result of alcohol or a breach of respect toward Thais. Thailand is no exception to a criminal underbelly (*mostly in Bangkok, Pattaya, and Koh Phangan*) involving drugs, prostitution, and human trafficking. Unless you're in the market for drugs, prostitutes, or human trafficking, you shouldn't run into trouble. If your idea of a good time is to go get hammered around brothels, hire and fail to pay prostitutes, then you most certainly will be introduced to another side of the Thai culture.

The police play an interesting role in crime. Many take bribes for minor traffic offenses. For example, I've known expats who have been given a fine for not wearing a helmet on a motorbike. They simply slid the officer $7 and it went away versus paying the $14 fine. The Tourist Police are friendly and somewhat helpful, although they know more about how to file your insurance claim than actually recouping your stolen goods.

Thais follow laws differently then what we are accustomed to in the Western world. It wouldn't be right to call Thailand lawless, just different. Many expats opt to do as the Thais do. The police often turn their heads if you're driving the wrong way down a motorway, but a foreigner caught with drugs, drunk, or causing physical harm (especially to a Thai) will be swiftly arrested, roughed up, and charged, not to mention assessed a hefty fine. If you're even considering participating in illegal activity, think twice. Watch the TV show "Locked Up Abroad," that should scare you out of doing something ill-advised.

✦Further TV homework: Watch *The Hangover: Part 2* for a comedic glimpse of Bangkok's dodgy side.

NIGHT LIFE

The night life in Thailand varies from city to city. Bars are the most common watering hole where everyone in the community mingles. There's at least one in every small town. You can find good ole' pubs in bigger cities and tourist hubs that are often

British or Irish themed and owned. A new Thai craze, *beer bars,* is springing up in the bigger cities offering an array of imported and exotic beers in addition to the usual Thai selections. Wine bars are also becoming more popular but are pricy for Thailand. An average glass of wine runs you 179 Bt ($6 USD). A pint of beer averages 100Bt ($3.30 USD).

There are two types of nightclubs in Thailand – Thai and *Farang* (foreigner). Generally speaking, Thais don't like to dance. They'd rather stand around tall cocktail tables and polish off a bottle of whiskey with their buddies. Foreigners are welcome in the Thai clubs, and are even occasionally offered drinks for free by customers as a friendly gesture. *Farang* nightclubs are where many expats end up, dancing and drinking into the wee hours of the morning. Like everyone's grandmother or grandfather has said, *"Nothing godly happens after midnight."* Farang nightclubs are often the *"store-front"* for prostitutes and drugs, so keep your wits.

SEX

To some, the mention of Thailand elicits images of beautiful beaches and temples. To others, it evokes images of famously gorgeous women. Sex tourism is common here, and unfortunately ,many men who travel to Thailand have hiring prostitutes on the 'to do' list. In addition to tourists, there are expats who clearly choose Thailand for the ladies of the night. They're commonly nicknamed *sexpats.* To those folks I would like to re-iterate most prostitutes are sex slaves illegally trafficked from neighboring Myanmar or Laos and are forced into the trade servicing up to ten men a night!

The legal age of consent is 15, which is often criticized as too young, and a contributor to the sex trade problem. Expats should take sexually transmitted diseases and HIV seriously. Outside of Bangkok, it's difficult to find doctors or clinics who can test for STD's, and some doctors seem reluctant to test for HIV. That means the local population certainly aren't testing! Officially, prostitution is illegal, but the law isn't enforced. Most hopping bars and nightclubs in the tourist district will have a few prostitutes.

✦Warning to all expats, especially men, who are new to Thailand: proceed with caution when picking up a girl at a bar. Due to rampant sex trafficking, you need to find a way to ask the delicate question, "Do I have to pay?"

Abortions are illegal but often performed. Condoms are easily purchased in 7-elevens, and many brands of birth control are available in pharmacies across the country without prescriptions. Plan B, or the morning after pill, is also available over the counter for less than $2!

The irony about romance in Thailand is while prostitution and sex is in your face anywhere you look, public affection is a bit of a taboo. Hand holding is the extent of "PDA" seen. I have *never* seen two Thai people kiss! Expats are somewhat exempt from the public affection ban but you may feel uncomfortable kissing in public because it will bring stares.

GAY / LESBIAN (LGBT)

Thailand is very LGBT friendly. There isn't a stigma or discrimination towards a person's choice of spouse. Some say this is because Thailand is a Buddhist country, but for whatever reason, the stigmas attached to sex and sexuality are not embedded in Thai culture. In fact, many younger Thai people are bi-sexual or gay. You'll rarely hear them label themselves as one or the other, however, because sexuality is not placed in a box like it is in the Western world.

A Thai student of mine once described the different types of sexual orientations, revealing to me a much more complex society than LGBT labels could cover. You'd need a lot more letters, I'll tell you that much! You have the heterosexual men and women, the toms (similar to lesbians but dress like boys and sometimes 'grow out of it'), the ladies who are straight but sometimes go with toms if they have no active part in sex, homosexual men, men who act extremely girly yet are straight, and then you have the gatoeys, a.k.a. lady boys. Gatoeys don't quite fit the transgender label but are so much more. In Thailand, you can never be sure if that beautiful woman sitting at the bar is actually a woman. I've heard many stories of drunken nights that ended with a surprise. Sexual diversity is taken light-heartedly and with a smile. See gay-thailand.net for more information.

RELIGION

Thailand is predominately a Buddhist country with 90-95% of the population identifying as Buddhist. In every town there's a Wat (temple) and monks wandering around in the mornings to collect their alms (food). Most Thai men ordain as a monk for a few weeks to bring merit to their parents and family, but some don't take it seriously. I've seen monks smoking or talking on a mobile phone to his girlfriend. I've met a few expats who've been ordained in their local monastery but this takes serious commitment. If this is a goal of yours, my advice would be to start by taking a meditation course at a monastery offering courses in English.

Thailand is very accepting of other religions which has led to Christian missionaries using Thailand as a base for other SE Asian countries (and China) for decades. As a result, many cities have churches of different denominations offering services in English, Thai, and (increasingly) Korean.

Many Thais assume that all Caucasian foreigners are Christian, because in the past, most of their visitors were, and it takes time for them to accept if you report that you are indeed a Buddhist. Some expats adopt Buddhism, while some pick and choose their favorite parts of the religion and ignore the rest, and others have nothing to do with Buddhism at all.

Thailand has a small population of Muslims, mostly concentrated in the southern provinces near the border with Malaysia. Pattani, Yala, and Narathiwat provinces are predominately Muslim and prone to insurgent attacks since the rebels want independence. Few expats choose to live in these provinces since the area is economically undeveloped, unstable, and generally unsafe.

FOOD & WATER

Thailand's tap water is not safe to drink, and occasionally pours out in a slightly brown hue. I've met expats with strong stomachs who drink it and who claim to have never had an issue. I wouldn't bet the ranch that the tap water will never do your intestines harm. I brush my teeth with tap water and have never experienced any problems. Filtered drinking water is readily available everywhere, from reverse osmosis filters to mineral, and even imported Evian bottles. Most apartment blocks and cities have refill stations. Place $.03 in one of these machines and it will yield a liter of filtered water. A 2L bottle (container) will run around .50 cents at a 7-Eleven.

Thailand's cuisine is famous around the world so expats are quite simply in food heaven! Thai food has a broad range of tastes, ingredients, and vegetables many expats have never seen before, so be prepared to try some new foods. Beware of the spice though, some dishes can blow you away! Painful to eat, and painful later. The spice index is usually marked on menus, so be vigilant.

Not only are there countless delicious Thai dishes, they are often dirt cheap ($1.10 – 3.10). Freshly cut seasonal fruit is a street favorite for expats. No longer do you have to spend your whole paycheck at Wholefoods for decent produce. Since Thailand is an international hub, it's also home to: every type of cuisine you can think of, international supermarkets, bakeries, pizza deliveries, burger joints, sushi, and in Bangkok, affordable Michelin-starred restaurants. In major cities, you'll find imported foods at comparable prices to home. Arguably, the most popular and missed food is cheese, but this can be bought or found in restaurants.

***Warning:** you're likely to gain weight from all the amazing food.

EXPAT EXPERIENCE

"The fruits are amazing, and on a hot, humid day, a juice always hits the spot. For those of you with a hangover, hello, fresh coconuts! Nature's best electrolyte replacement! A major favorite thing for me to do is simply walk down the street, surrounded by countless food stalls. Being able to stroll down and get fresh food regularly is amazing. Meat on a stick, and some sticky rice? Yes, please. It's a perfect grab and go meal. You need something sweet? Well here's a bag of fresh mango! Especially at a market, you'll be overwhelmed with choices of fresh mouth-watering delights, I know I was. There's always something there you haven't tried. My advice is be adventurous and try everything once. You never know, you could be missing out on your new favorite dish if you don't!"

~ Kayla Colyard, American, ESL Teacher

LANGUAGE

Thai is a tonal language closely related to Laoation, but not much else. If you're not from Lao then you don't have much of an advantage. Even the alphabet, their version of the "ABCs," looks like a complete mystery to a new expat. To make matters even more challenging, Thai includes a variety of dialects such as: Northern, Southern, and Issan. Bangkok/ Central Thai is the easiest to learn and everyone will understand it, that is, if you speak it correctly.

I strongly recommend learning some basic phrases in Thai. It will make life easier and greatly improve your interactions with Thai people. Many expats skip this step, deeming it unnecessary because their English is understood. You can virtually do everything in Thailand without Thai. Every restaurant has an English menu, banks have an English speaker, heck, even the police hire expats to help them communicate in tourist areas. Just because you don't have to learn Thai, doesn't mean you shouldn't learn some basics.

EXPAT EXPERIENCE

How much of a difference does being fluent in Thai make to your daily life? I know many expats who speak little Thai and get by fine, but I'm interested what it's like to understand everything?

"Being able to speak, read, and write Thai has afforded me several benefits. First, I'm able to get around with relative ease and don't have to rely on anyone to read and explain documents. I work for the Thai government and have to use Thai daily not only for myself but to assist my other foreign colleagues. It also allows me to make friends with Thais more easily. I'm able to understand the news and politics.

Knowing Thai allows people to be more comfortable talking to you. Many Thais are too shy to speak English so allowing them to speak Thai, make jokes in Thai, really allows them to be at ease and have a conversation with someone that they may not have ever had the opportunity.

On the other hand, I've had the unfortunate experience of hearing things that are either blatantly ignorant, false or both. So it exposes you to all things good and bad about this country."

~ Aaron Johnson, American, Legal Professional

The tones seem to stump many people. *Khaow* can mean rice, white, news, or he/she! Not to fret, you're not in it alone if you don't want to be! There are many language schools and private teachers available. Many expats learn the alphabet by themselves and *Thai for Beginners* is a good book to start with.

Another good way to learn is by dating a Thai. Romance can be the necessary motivating ingredient to push you to speak intermediate or advanced Thai.

CLIMATE

Since the land spans over such a large space, the weather can vary drastically. In general, there are three seasons: hot, less hot, and rainy. *"Newbee"* expats may find the hot and rainy seasons challenging, but veterans who've grown accustomed to the changes barely notice the difference.

Season	Period	Characteristics	Potential Problems
Hot	Mar - May	Temperatures to 95 F (35c) and above. High humidity in Bangkok and central areas (cooler along the coast due to wind).	Little rainfall, therefore high risk for forest fires. Avoid going out midday, take care to drink enough water. It's dry and dusty.
Cold	Oct - Feb	Cool temperatures, dry, usually clear blue skies and green forests. The North and North East are cooler than the South	Cold snaps occur around December. Thai houses are built for hot weather, in the North it can get very cold! Bangkok and the South rarely drop below 68F (20C)

Season	Period	Characteristics	Potential Problems
Rainy	June - Sept	Heavy rainfall and monsoons. The rain varies from heavy, short downpours, to continuous rainfall lasting up to two weeks. When it's not raining, it's sunny and fresh.	Flooding can damage houses, especially roofs, as well as halt a city (see Bangkok flooding in 2011). The humidity brings mold, a source of complaint for many expats. Take care to air out your rooms regularly (dehumidifiers are rarely used and expensive). Mosquitoes breed more during rainy season, increasing the risk of Malaria and Dengue fever (see *Healthcare* for more information).

> **TIP**
>
> You'll notice that Thailand runs on its own schedule. People are often late without apology. Buses will arrive when they arrive, 4pm means anytime between 4pm and 5pm, and if you are late, mai pen rai (it doesn't matter). Similar to the Italian and Spanish Mediterranean time, some attribute this to warm weather or culture, but once you've been stuck in a rainy season downpour and were faced with the choice to go outside or be late, you'll begin to understand the reason for Thai time.

NATURE

The nature in Thailand is truly stunning. From the mountains of the North, elephants, wildlife, waterfalls, and rice paddies, to the picture-perfect islands, crystal clear water, marine life, coral and stunning beaches. The only thing that's missing is snow. Thailand boasts over 100 national parks, and yet there are still hundreds of additional beautiful spots slowly creeping onto the tourist track. To support the growing tourism industry, forests are being leveled for new hotel construction.

Community parks are few and far apart, since most Thais would prefer air-conditioning above a walk in the oppressive heat-filled nature. Luckily, many ancient trees in the cities have been blessed by monks who wrap a colorful fabric around the trunk, ensuring they are preserved and not cut down. Despite urbanization, nature is easily accessed within one hour from any major city *(even Bangkok where Kanchanaburi and its forest is about an hour outside the capital)*. Conservation groups, and other attempts toward conservation, perma-culture, and organic farming are on the rise.

TRANSPORTATION

Thailand offer more modes of transportation than you could imagine: buses, motorbikes, mini-vans, tuk-tuks (motorcycle taxi with a carriage for additional seating), and even elephants! I would hazard a guess that it's one of the easiest countries to travel around. Each mode of transit has a different level of comfort. See below for more information about transportation options.

LONG DISTANCE

Airplane

Bangkok's international airport (Suvarnabhumi) offers flights to over 120 destinations, and is the most connected airport in SE Asia! Domestically, Thailand is home to many cost efficient airlines, connecting the country by air from Suvarnabhumi or Don

Muang airport to any of the 63 domestic destinations. The low-cost airlines also connect Thailand to neighboring countries such as: Myanmar, Malaysia, Singapore, and even further to China and Hong Kong. This is great news for those who'd like to explore Asia on the cheap.

Check <u>Air Asia</u>, <u>Nok air</u>, and <u>Bangkok airways</u> for cheap flights.

Bus

Buses serve all major towns, cities, and tourist destinations in Thailand. They run day and night with different class options: VIP, 1st class, 2nd class, government, and local. VIP offers you dinner, snacks and drinks on-board, while the local bus opens their windows for "air-conditioning" and offer enough leg room for a toddler, a very short toddler.

To give you an idea of expense: 1st class BKK- Chiang Mai runs around $27, BKK- Krabi $30. Thirty bucks will get you to most major cities. In my opinion, 1st or 2nd class is usually a comfortable ride. <u>Green Bus</u>,[5] <u>NakhonChai Air</u>,[6] and <u>Sombat Tours</u> (website is in Thai)[7] are the best companies to travel with. They each have websites to check times and destinations, and their VIP services are worth the extra expense.

You want a real adventure and opportunity to be immersed in the culture you say? Local buses cost next to nothing and are often piled high with rice, vegetables, and locals headed to the market. You might be the only expat / foreigner on the bus, so expect some curious stares and questions.

TIP

To avoid theft, take buses directly from the bus station and one full of Thai people! Some tourist buses attract locals who rummage through the suitcases and bags stored below the bus. They'll take anything resellable. I once lost a memory stick, book, and a t-shirt. Gives a new meaning to rummage sale, eh?

Minivan

Silver vans equipped with 9-12 seats serve shorter distances (2-3 hours) and are usually faster than buses. Common minivan routes include: Phuket – Krabi and Bkk – Kanchanaburi. They're also used for visa runs, see *Perpetual* Tourism in the *Immigration* section for more information.

Train

There's a train that runs the entire length of Thailand. It can be a nice alternative to flying or the bus (with a similar pricetag).

---

[5] http://bus.greencorporatethai.com/

[6] http://www.nakhonchaiair.com/ncabooking/frm_accept.php

[7] http://www.sombattour.com/html/home.php

Traveling on the train is not the norm, and sometimes stations are outside of city centers. Chiang Mai to Bangkok route is known for delays, so I wouldn't recommend it if you're in a rush. Bangkok headed to the South is much more reliable, since it's served by faster, newer trains.

SHORT DISTANCE / CITY TRANSPORT

Tuk - Tuk

Taxi

This is the first kind of transportation you will encounter at the airports. Taxis start at $1.10 in Bangkok. Some cabs offer a fixed price to various destinations in the city. Taxi drivers' English range from fluent to zero. A good rule of thumb is to print directions to your hotel in Thai or show them on a map. Cities along the tourist track have no shortage of cabs. Request to use the meter, some taxis offer a set price but it's usually higher than the metered price. If the driver insists the meter *is broken today,* then I'll usually decline and flag down another.

Tuk-tuk

If you can't find a taxi don't worry, there will be a tuk-tuk waiting. Drivers happily follow foreigners around shouting "tuk-tuk," possibly making them the most annoying thing about Thailand. They'll offer you a set price, but feel free to haggle. Tuk-tuk's are loud, usually contain disco lights, and drive erratic but are something everybody needs to experience at least once; just hold on!

Songthaew

A red *shared* taxi with two rows of seats in the back of the truc, songthaew's are the cheapest type of Taxi (usually $0.60) because you have to share it with other people and passengers who depart one by one. They're not as comfortable as air-conditioned taxis and drivers rarely speak English, so it's best to tell them a well known landmark to get to your destination. Sometimes on short routes songthaews will be used instead of a bus. They roam all over, and in the daytime are often more available than taxis or tuk-tuks. You'll know they're around because they beep their horn when approaching anyone walking to show their presence. This is almost as annoying as the tuk-tuks.

Sky Train / Metro

Bangkok is the only city with an extensive metro system, however, it doesn't reach the outskirts of the city. Bangkok also has city buses but it's a nightmare to work out routes and you won't find English translations on any of the maps. If you're seeking an adventure, I dare you to hop on one and see where you go.

TIP
Wear shoes that you can easily remove, and travel light when island hopping, since you often wade in knee deep water to board your boat. You will have to carry your suitcase and your shoes to the boat!

Boats

There's an extensive boat network shuttling people to the islands. You can purchase a combination bus + boat ticket to places like Koh Samui and Koh Chaang. When purchasing ahead, however, it's virtually impossible to know what kind of boat you'll get. Prices to island hop can be drastically different, so shop around.

PRIVATE TRANSPORT

When you first arrive, a combination of your own two feet and public transportation will likely suffice, but after awhile many expats opt to rent or buy their own form of transport for the added independence, comfort, and ease.

Motorbike

The most common form of personal travel in Thailand is motorbike. They're cheap to rent $100 per month, easy to drive, allow you to zip through traffic, and is super fun! Driving a motorbike is straightforward, and while you're more vulnerable, cars are accustomed to looking out for you.

You drive on the *left* in Thailand. Once you're familiar with Thai driving, however, you'll notice that locals don't stick to just the left-hand side. Locals even drive along walkways if traffic is bad. You can weave through traffic, park almost everywhere, and turn around on a dime on a motorbike. Thai-style driving is very relaxed about rules. Choose your level of compliance at your own risk.

There are a few downsides to motorbikes: you are exposed to the sun and rain, and accidents on a bike are far worse than accidents in cars. Foreigners can drive motorbikes with any international recognized license (no motorcycle endorsement needed). After six months, to remain legal you need to take a Thai driving test. There are expats that drag their feet satisfying this requirement with the excuse that if the police can be appeased with a small bribe, why go through the trouble? Read more about driving requirements in the *After You Arrive* section.

Car

If you prefer the comfort and safety of a car, they can be rented or bought with relatively ease. As a foreigner, cars are usually purchased up front in cash, so make sure you check the car carefully before buying. Google maps has extensive coverage of Thailand so navigation is simple as long as you have a smart device with cellular connection.[8] Cars are subject to heavy traffic in the big cities and parking can be a pain, Bangkok being the worst! Most Thais drive 4x4s or trucks even though the main roads and highways in Thailand are decent. The high action and 4x4 are helpful during heavy rainfalls and flooding. For more information about bringing your car or buying one, see the *Logistics* section.

---

[8] see the **Communication** section for more information

Bicycle

Many expats opt for this two-wheeled option to get some exercise while traveling from point A to B.

IDENTIFICATION

Officially you should carry your passport or a copy at all times, however, in three years I've only been asked once or twice to show it. Each time I was on a bus to a border area where police check for undocumented immigrants. Take care with your passport, they're a hot commodity in Bangkok's black market.

Looking like a foreigner offers you advantages and disadvantages. Locals can spot you a mile away, greet you in English, and treat you like a tourist even if you can speak fluent Thai. Foreigners rarely need to show ID, since they blend in with tourists. If you're Asian, they'll assume you're Thai. Asian friends of mine are sometimes irritated by this. On the upside, speaking or looking Thai grants you discounts and *Thai prices*! Tuk-tuk drivers, in particular, try to gouge foreigners in the hope that you're fresh off of the plane, and $10 sounds reasonable for a 10 minute journey when it should really cost $3. Whether you pay more for a cab or merchandise, prices are all given in good faith with wide smiles. (Read more about estimated expenses in the *Cost of Living* section).

EXPAT EXPERIENCE

A love letter to Thailand:

"I love taking the boat out and exploring the bays and neighboring islands. I love never being cold (except in the cinema). I love the beaches and the fact that you don't have to pack a thing to go to the beach other than your towel, as deck chairs and food vendors are available. Of course, if you want a quiet beach on Samui, it's not a far drive to the quieter side of the island. I love the fresh fruit and cheap cocktails and walking the street market. I admire the way Thai people pick themselves up after a disaster and get back to life (such as after the floods on the island in November 2010 and again in March 2011). I love how therapeutic it seems for Thai people to sweep – it almost seems like a national pastime. There's always somebody sweeping with a smile on their face, with those lovely fan-shaped brooms... such a silly little thing to love! I love an ice-cold fresh coconut to drink... should I go on...?

Of course, there are things I miss, in particular friends and family, and some home comforts, but weighing out the good with the bad, and there's no doubt that we made the right decision to move. They say that once Africa is in your blood, you'll always love it, and it's true. I do miss Africa, but I love Asia just as much, and I call Thailand home now. I don't feel that a person has to be tied down to a country their whole life, or feel like they've 'deserted' their old country by enjoying a new one."

~ Rosanne

IMMIGRATION

Getting here is easy, staying here is the tricky part

Expats come to Thailand with a variety of goals in mind. Some live it up, while others do as little as possible. Stress-free living with sunshine and great food is on everyone's list. I'll admit, life here is great for expats, as long as they can figure out a way to live here long-term. A feat that proves to be tricky for some.

Some expats, particularly those without pensions, can encounter visa *issues* during their stay. Most of these issues are solved by throwing time, travel, or money at them. If you ever need an ice-breaker at an expat hotspot, bring up visas and you're sure to hear some stories. It seems like everyone has a '*nightmare at the embassy*' story to share. I've been in Thailand for over three years and since I've changed jobs so many times, I've grown an impressive collection of visas varying in type and length. Visas in Thailand are actually quite straightforward, but almost always require planning and travel to a Thai embassy abroad. No matter which visa is right for you, be prepared for check-ins every 90 days or so, because the majority of visas require it.

In mid-2014, yet another government coup occurred in Thailand. While coup has negative associations, the military and General in charge have been working hard to ensure the country is functioning and progressing. One issue they've been addressing is illegally working on tourist visas. The visa rules and loopholes are slowly being closed, but the basics laid out in this section still hold true. (Check our website for updates regarding www.becominganexpat.com)

UPON ARRIVAL

If you are a citizen from Western countries and arrive by air, you're automatically granted a 30 day stamp in your passport. Passport holders from Brazil, Chile, Argentina, Korea, and Peru are awarded 90 days. In the recent past, most nationalities entering Thailand by land were only granted a 15 day stamp. However, in November of 2013, Thailand announced that citizens of the UK, USA, Japan, Germany, France, Canada and Italy would be given a 30 stamp when arriving by land. The extra two weeks eases the time crunch between switching visas, a benefit I've already taken advantage of.

Shortly after the land visas were extended, the Thai government changed the rules allowing only one "border run" and is being enforced at the borders. The changes were made to deter perpetual tourism and force more folks to purchase visas.

PERPETUAL TOURIST

A perpetual tourist is someone who doesn't have an extended visa, they live in Thailand on their *tourist visa* by renewing their entrance stamp every 15-90 days, depending on their country of origin. Some people refer to the practice as a loop-hole in the immigration rules, others call it mis-leading because you check the *tourist* box when you clearly live in Thailand. This book does not condone the practice, it simply acknowledges that it exists.

TIP
Visa/Border Run
This term may be new to you. It refers to the practice that many perpetual tourists use to maintain their visa requirements. Sometimes expats combine runs with a holiday or chance to see a neighboring country. Other times expats go and return in one long day on the bus.
A border run is where you travel to one of the many border checkpoints, exit Thailand, enter another country, have lunch, go shopping at the border market, and then re-enter Thailand, activating a new visa which permits you another 15, 30, or 90 day stamp in your passport. Re-entering Thailand is free, but when you exit, you must enter another country (Myanmar, Laos, Cambodia or Malaysia- all bar Malaysia require you to buy a visa). There are numerous companies that offer transport for border runs. From the south, Malaysia or Ranong,Myanmar are the easiest crossings. From Chiang Mai and the north, Mai Sai is hassle free, and the Issan region has good access to Laos crossings. Expats in Bangkok usually fly out on cheap flights.

TOURIST VISA

Tourist Visas are obtained at any <u>Thai embassy</u>[9] and are valid for 60 days, you can request a single, double, or triple entry. Double or triple requests sometimes require you to furnish proof of flights but other times saying, "I'm taking a bus to Cambodia" satisfies them. Average cost per entry is $40 USD but embassies vary, each entry can be extended by 30 days with a visit to an immigration officen within Thailand.

I've known folks who've lived in Thailand over three years on tourist visas, and while he or she may not be working, they certainly don't classify as a tourist. These are rare cases, however, because once you have *"too many"* tourist visa stamps in your passport, many embassies will refuse to issue new ones. The Thai embassies in Kuala Lumpur, Penang, Malaysia, and Singapore are hesitant to give out Education or double/triple entry tourist visas.

If you have no official work in Thailand, e.g. if you're writing a book, working online (digital nomads), an artist, or just hanging out, then a tourist or education visa will be your best bet.

NON-IMMIGRANT VISA

Foreigners who wish to live long-term, work, or invest in Thailand must apply for a Non-Immigrant Visa. Non-immigrant visas are initially valid as a single entry (90 days) but can be converted to one year once in the country. If you have a one year visa, you still need to report to the immigration office every 90 days. There are a variety of categories, each limited for specific goals. See the following table.

---

[9] http://www.thaiembassy.org/main/

Visa	Expat Situation
F	To perform official duties
B	Conduct business, to work, to study teaching course, to work as an English teacher, to take scuba diving or boxing lessons, to work as a sport coach, to do an internship, to work as a film-producer, journalist or reporter for a short period (up to 3 years).
IM	To invest with the concurrence of the Thai Ministries and Government Departments concerned.
ED	To study, to come on a work study tour or observation tour, to participate in projects or seminars, to attend a conference or training course, to study as a foreign Buddhist monk.
M	To work as a film-producer, journalist or reporter.
R	To perform missionary work or other religious activities with the concurrence of the Thai Ministries or Government Departments concerned.
RS	To conduct scientific research or training or teaching in a research institute.
EX	To undertake skilled work or to work as an expert or specialist.
O	To visit Thai spouse, children, parents, voluntary job, Retirement (with State Pension)
O-A	To applicants aged 50 and over who wish to stay in Thailand for an extended period without the intention of working (one year renewable).

RETIREMENT: O-A LONG STAY

The O-A is the clear choice for those in retirement. See the requirements below:

✦You're at least 50 years young
✦You can prove a monthly income or pension of approximately $2,000, drop $25,000 in a Thai bank account, or a combination of the two
✦Hand over a clean criminal record and medical certificate
✦Obtain the O-A visa outside of Thailand
✦Report to immigration office (or do a border run) every 90 days
✦If an accompanying spouse doesn't qualify for the O-A visa, they can apply for an *accompanying spouse* visa.

NON-IMMIGRANT B TYPES

B is for Business and B is needed for anyone who wants to conduct business, work, invest, or teach in Thailand. To get a non-B, you'll need a sponsor company or school who will prepare corporate documents to accompany the visa application. Once you secure a non-B visa, you'll need to apply for the accompanying work permit (to work legally, you need both the non-B visa and a work permit). The company or school hiring you should sort the paperwork for you.

Your type of business will determine what extra paperwork will need to be submitted:

◆Work for hire: Letter of invitation from a company qualified to employ foreigners
◆Business: Document showing correspondence with trading partners in Thailand, balance sheet, and a statement of income tax
◆Investment: Letter from Thailand's Board of Investment
◆English teacher: Copy of your degree and teaching certificate

Like most countries, Thailand has laws to protect jobs for its citizens. There are very few circumstances where a company is permitted to hire a foreigner, it must be proven that a Thai person isn't capable of doing the job. Teaching English for example, should be done by a native English speaker. Other common expat jobs exist in: tourism, exports, and IT. If a specialized skill isn't proven, then the Thai company is only permitted one foreign employee for every $61,415 in capital and must maintain a 6:1 thai : foreigner employment ratio.

If you're planning on starting a business, I really recommend you take your time, find legal assistance, learn the market, and the Thai culture. I've met many expats who've attempted to start a restaurant or import business only to fail as the demand couldn't support it. Read more about starting a business in the **Work Hard Play Hard** section.[10]

---

[10] The Thai Embassy website offers a basic guide to starting a business in Thailand www.thaiembassy.com/business/business_forming.php

---

TIP

Any non-immigrant visa can be turned into a non-B visa. Sometimes employers will ask you to work under your current visa (non-ED or non-O) then when it expires, they will help you change your visa. This is not advised and is not legal. It's worth the time and hassle to follow the rules. After teaching in Thailand for a year, I applied for a job in Japan, and they required a copy of my Thai work visa and permit. I was glad that I pushed my employer to give me one despite their reluctance (and my $300 for the visa and permit).

NON-IMMIGRANT - O TYPES

The O officially stands for *other,* but a common nickname among the expat community is *ordeal.* You aren't working, you aren't studying, you aren't a tourist, you are other, undefined. Today, O is split up to represent retirement, marriage, accompanying family members, medical treatments, volunteer, or social work.

MARRIAGE (to a Thai National)

This route requires the following additional documents:

✦Marriage certificate
✦Wife / husband's house registration and identity card
✦Sometimes you need to show a letter to certify a monthly salary of over $12,400 in a Thai bank account
✦If you have a Thai child, you can also apply for a dependency visa. You'll need their birth certificate

Marriage is one route taken by older expats who don't qualify for the retirement visas. Marrying for love, companionship, and convenience.

ACCOMPANYING SPOUSE OR FAMILY

✦Relatively easy for accompanying spouses and children to obtain if their partner is coming for a job and will get a non-B visa supplied. (If you are coming to find a job, then your partner is better off getting a Tourist visa.)

✦You should apply for all the visas together (ideally at your home embassy to make things easier), and be able to show funds to support the accompanying family members

✦Marriage certificate and birth certificate for children

✦Accompanying family can work in Thailand on this visa with a valid work permit

It's fairly easy for children to secure visas. If you've already chosen a school, they will provide all the necessary paperwork for your child's non-immigrant visa. However, to get the paperwork, the school usually requires the tuition upfront. Some schools require your child to have a visa already, be it a single entry, education, or a non-O visa. See the *Family and Education* section for more information.

VOLUNTEERING

Here are the additional forms needed to volunteer:

✦A letter from an NGO (non-governmental organization) that is registered in Thailand. Very few NGO's are actually officially registered, so if you plan on volunteering for a short time, it's easier to apply for a tourist visa.

✦In the past, this was a very easy visa but in 2012, they started to clamp down on volunteers. Today, a 1 year volunteer visa is a rare occurrence. If you do manage to secure this visa, a one year will actually give you 15 months (if you do a border run the day before it expires).

NON-IMMIGRANT – ED

Another way to stay in Thailand without working is the Education visa. If you want to study Thai, attend a training course, enroll as a Buddhist monk, or even learn Muay Thai, you need to apply for a non-ED. Most of the time, the language school or training gym will help you secure this visa as part of a package. However, only registered institutions are actually able to issue non-ED visa paperwork (and official invitation letters). If you are after the non-ED as a means to stay in the country, check out popular year long offers from a variety of language schools. The cost averages $800-1,000. For those who don't qualify for the retirement visa and who'd like to learn something while they're in the country, this is a great deal. The visa can be extended for up to 5 years. Make sure you attend classes because after three years, immigration police may test your Thai skills.

EXPAT EXPERIENCE

"The biggest problems I've had with visas have been in-between longer term visas, when I've been on 15 days on arrival. I chose to get the Education visa partly to get rid of the hassle of doing visa runs and going to immigration to pay for extensions, but mainly because I wanted to speed up the process of learning Thai. The education visa gets you up to 15 months in total + around 200 hours of Thai classes. You are required to check in with immigration every 3 months to update your address, but it doesn't seem to be a problem. In my case, I took the Thai course in Krabi, and they are fine with me checking into immigration anywhere in Thailand so long as I do it every three months."

~ Johan Pellsater, Sweden

OTHER TYPES

There are other visas such as journalist, scientific research, missionary, diplomat and official but these are given case by case. Should you need one of these, it's best to email a <u>Thai embassy</u> for further information.

TIP
If you plan to travel out of Thailand (once or often), you need to get a re-entry permit to avoid a single entry visa getting cancelled. You can apply at an immigration office or at Suvarnabhumi International Airport before leaving the country.

Immigration here is tricky, don't be afraid to ask expats or your immigration attorney for clarification.

TIP
If you overstay any visa, there is a daily fine of $15.35 with a max of $615!

WHAT REGION IS BEST FOR YOU?

Guiding you to your slice of heaven

So you settled on a country, you're in good company! In 2013, Thailand topped <u>HSBC's Expat survey</u>[11] for best overall experience in South East Asia. Thailand scored especially high in getting settled, financial security, integrating, and finding friends. Before coming to Thailand, I didn't know what to expect. I envisioned drunk Brits on a beach *(like those in Koh Phangan)*, older sexpats with young Thai girls *(unfortunately, I can also find that in most large cities)*, and pensioners looking for an economic way to live out their golden years. What surprised me was the size of the young ambitious population, beautiful scenery, diversity of climates, and diversity of expats.

It was hard to take in so much information and decide on a city to settle in. It can be overwhelming trying to choose between the beach, nature, night life, shopping, and culture. It's like the

---

[11] (http://blogs.wsj.com/searealtime/2013/10/30/foreign-workers-say-thailand-is-tops/

cereal aisle in a large North American grocery store, too many choices is not always good. Don't worry, I'll help you whittle down your options.

I quickly fell in love with the small and energetic Chiang Mai in the north after a week-long visit. It's home to the perfect balance of nature and city with friendly people and a rich culture. However, some friends of mine have visited and wonder why I'm here, calling it boring, full of traffic, and touristy.

Thailand's cities are diverse, each with its own personality and vibe. Unless you move for work, I suggest you visit and stay a month in a few different cities before you commit to one. While visiting each region, keep in mind what is important to you. Common needs include: particular climate, western-styled accommodations , close proximity to the airport, certain mix of activities (such as hiking, beach walks, birding, kayaking, etc), and social outlets.

Let's take a look at the major expat hubs in Thailand and shop for your next hometown.

CENTRAL THAILAND

BANGKOK

While there's a scattering of foreigners across the country, a huge chunk of them live and work in Bangkok. The retired expat and digital nomads are afforded more freedom to wander throughout Thailand.

Bangkok is home to a rotating population of 8-14 million people. It's home to jobs with the highest wages (due to a higher cost of living), 5 star restaurants, western-styled shopping, and a lively night life. Bangkok certainly earned its capital status.

Like most large cities, Bangkok has a variety of suburbs, all with their own feel. You could rent a sky scraper apartment with a rooftop pool, or walk a block down the same street and lease a traditional wooden home with your own chickens in the garden.

Traveling within Bangkok is time consuming and a big part of expat life. Taxis are everywhere, but so is traffic. There's a sky train and a metro which are cheap and fast, but they don't connect the entire city. Many people use a combination of both types of transport to get to their destination. If you elect to work, make sure you live close to your job or your morning commute could last upwards of two hours.

EXPAT EXPERIENCE

"Bangkok - family first and the educational opportunities here far exceed anywhere else in Thailand, also socially this is where my friends and social life are. I don't have a great deal to do with the so called expat community and most of my social activities revolve around either my wife's work friends or airline schedules as most of my friends are pilots (Thai). I also fly and am hoping that at least one of the twins also takes up the profession. This also gives me cause for further comment as the local university has just spent $17 million installing a real flight simulator, no uni that I know of in Australia has this!"

~ Chris Taylor, Australian/British, Engineer

WEATHER

Bangkok is hot all year-round. Temperatures hover between 82 F - 100 F, or 28 - 38 C. The rainy season (June - September) is welcomed and scorned because with it come more traffic and delays, but on the positive side, it cools and cleans the city.

THINGS TO DO

Bangkok has so much to offer: culture, live music, IMAX cinemas, poetry readings, shows, wine bars, golf courses (including one between the runways of Don Muang Airport), language schools, meet up groups, expat groups, and shopping malls. It's a wonderful blend of culture and western amenities. There is never a dull moment!

WHERE TO LIVE

Accommodations range from small bedsit with a squat toilet to luxurious penthouses and everything in-between. Bangkok is the most expensive city in Thailand, but if money isn't an issue, you can find some amazing properties. Most foreigners live in condominiums with pools or in comfortable western-style houses.

PROXIMITY TO AIRPORT

Bangkok has two airports in the city, Mueang International Airport and Suvarnabuhmi Airport, with low-cost domestic and international flights to hundreds of worldwide destinations! Suvarnabuhmi Airport is even connected to the city centre by the sky train. If airport proximity ranks high on your priorities, then Bangkok could be your slice.

SOCIAL REQUIREMENTS

If you enjoy a fast pace of life, wining and dining, enjoying the company of friends, and Hi-So (a *Tinglish*[12] term meaning high society), then Bangkok is the place for you. Making expat friends

---

[12] like spanglish, a mix of Thai and English

is a breeze with the plethora of social events and hobby clubs in Bangkok. If you enjoy nature, fresh air, and hate traffic then *avoid* Bangkok. I used to be intimidated by Bangkok because of the stories I'd heard and the expansiveness of the city. Now that I've taken the time to explore Bangkok, I really enjoy spending a few days in such a stimulating and animated city.

TIP
To distinguish expats from tourists, look at their clothing. If there's an elephant pattern or a beer Chaang t-shirt, they're more than likely a tourist. If they're dressed in business wear, jeans, long sleeves or don't appear to be sweating profusely, they're probably an expat.

PATTAYA

If you travel two hours southwest of Bangkok, you'll arrive at Pattaya, home to beaches, babes, and a bad reputation. Many of the expats who live in Pattaya are there for the ladies. There are prostitutes everywhere, so if that bothers you, don't go. It's home to the bustling sex industry, lady boys, and Russian gangsters. In addition to the strip joints, bars, clubs, and restaurants, is an enormous floating market. There's also an incredible wooden temple overlooking the sea, shops, and excellent eateries.

If you enjoy the area, but the sex industry is a bit overwhelming to you, take the inexpensive ferry to nearby Koh Larn, an island just off the coast of Pattaya.

"It's a great escape! A small island were the sex industry is less in your face. The beach is calm and the water is beautiful. If you need an escape from the mainland, definitely head here!"

~ Kayla Colyard, ESL Teacher, Chonburi

★**Men beware:** walk down the wrong road in Pattaya and it'll be hard to stop the women from touching and pulling you into their bars. Sounds nice but most men I've spoken with tell me it was annoying to be seen merely as money.

★**Women beware:** you might be put off by the objectification of women, who stroll the town in next to nothing.

Weather

A cool breeze from the coast offers a slight relief to the stifling heat of Thailand. The rainy season starts around May and lasts through September. December offers the best weather here.

What to Do

By far the most active "to do" options here are: night gogo bars, strip teases, and hitting the clubs. By day, check out the beautiful beaches and nearby villages.

Accommodations

You can rent anything from a studio apartment to a large home. Some perpetual tourists opt to rent a hotel room long term. Wherever you stay, if you plan to have late night visitors make sure the management is okay with it, otherwise you might get kicked out!

Proximity to Airport

The U-TAPAO international airport is located 40 kilometers outside of Pattaya. However if you're flying internationally, it's often cheaper to fly into Bangkok's Suvarnabhumi Airport and hire a shuttle to transfer you the two hours to Pattaya.

Social Requirements

Enjoying a drink and an open opinion about sexuality, along with a dose of humor, is all that's needed to make friends in Pattaya. Don't expect these friendships to be deep-rooted as you often don't learn their real names, or connect with them outside of Pattaya. However, there are exceptions to every rule.

Hua Hin

Hua Hin is fit for a king, no really it's where the King of Thailand's current home is located. Hua Hin is an upscale beach resort area that attracts Thais who enjoy boutique hotels and high-priced restaurants, and expats who enjoy luxury for a fraction of the cost to North America. Hua Hin does an extraordinary job filtering out the negative aspects of Thailand. Compared to other beach scenes, the nightlife in Hua Hin is a more relaxed 'beer by the beach' fare.

Weather

An average of 82 F, 28 C. Remarkably cooler than Bangkok, and most accommodations are climate-controlled. Hua Hin is said to have the **best weather in Thailand**: not too hot, not too rainy. No wonder the King lives there!

What to Do

With an influx of Bangkokians traveling to Hua Hin to enjoy a weekend escape, it's rapidly becoming more touristy. This is good and bad. With tourism, comes activities: golf, water sports, fishing, jungle treks, and more. An increase in tourism will bring forth more crowds as well, but it's not inundated just yet. In addition to exciting activities, there is excellent shopping and cuisine available here.

Where to Live

You have many options here ranging from a condominium complex with a private pool and massive sea views, to a quaint house in a gated community. Part-time expats often decide to rent a hotel room long-term.

Proximity to Airport

Hua Hin Airport (HHQ) flies to Bangkok, Phuket, Samui, and Singapore but flights are a bit pricy. Shuttles and mini-vans depart regularly from Bangkok's Suvarnabhumi Airport to Hua Hin, so with a two hour drive you can save some cash.

Social Requirements

Hua Hin is populated with a large retiree expat crowd and affluent Thai. Stability and stress-free are commodities valued higher than adrenaline and extreme sports. Expats are often respectable, educated folks, which isn't the norm for a Thai beach town.

Nakon Sawan

Nakon Sawan is located smack in the middle of Thailand. It's home to a healthy established expat community – mostly consisting of English teachers and business men with Thai wives. The city looks a bit generic lacking special charm but has all of the basic amenities an expat could need. However, it's not geared toward Western life.

Accommodations are cheap in Nakon Sawan – A 2 bedroom house rents for $330. It's a good base for exploring Thailand with Bangkok's airport an hour and a half away. It's also a huge hub for cross-country buses. The expat social scene is small, so if a thriving social life is what you seek, this might not be the place for you.

THE NORTH

Chiang Mai

Often nicknamed the jewel of the north, Chiang Mai, is a city loved by many. About 20 years ago, CM was a sleepy little town built around an old city and a moat. Today, the old city still exists with the ruins adjacent to guest houses, tour companies, and other tourists infrastructure. The city has undergone large expansions, including the addition of apartment blocks and shopping malls. You can guess how the expansion has affected traffic. CM is an affordable city which draws in a large expat crowd.

Accessing nature, namely breath-taking mountains is a synch. Overlooking the city is the impressive Doi Suthep mountain and temple.

Weather

Cooler than most of Thailand, in December pants and socks are needed. Due to urban growth, deforestation has lead to an increasingly warm summer. The rainy season is moderate compared to other parts of Thailand. Local tribes have a burn season March - April which significantly decreases the air quality during those months. Some days it's so bad you can't see the mountain. Oftentimes, expats who aren't bound by work take this time of year to explore other regions.

What to Do

Get lost. CM has endless small, winding streets that are bound to lead you astray. Getting lost can lend you to some amazing places and pockets of culture around each turn. If you're looking for a hobby or new trade, the money you save with the cheap cost of living in CM can afford you classes in: massage, Thai boxing, Thai language, and yoga. Chiang Mai is also riddled with cafes which suits expats who work online.

Where to Live

Younger expats often live in studio apartments from $123 per month! Expats with families, and retirees, usually opt for an American-styled rental home or a home in a gated community (*moo baans*) with a shared pool.

Proximity to Airport

The Chang Mai Airport (CNX) is an international airport reachable in 20 minutes or less from anywhere in the city. The downside is the arriving and departing planes pollute the city with thunderous jet engine noise.

Social Requirements

Chang Mai is a revolving door when it comes to expats. One reason is the high population of part-time expats. This could result in the need to cultivate new friendships regularly.

If you're a night owl and enjoy disco-techs, CM's three clubs might leave you disappointed. For many, however, this place has more than enough to keep them entertained and fulfilled.

Chiang Rai

A smaller version of Chiang Mai, Chiang Rai is a sleepy authentic Thai town with some impressive temples and mountain scenery. Don't expect much going on here. CR is usually treated as a weekend getaway, but those who desire a bit of privacy will find beauty everywhere and easily make themselves at home.

Pai

Pai is a hippie-flavored mountain town. If the sixties were your best years, feel free to re-live them here. The small town was discovered by foreigners over 20 years ago. Most visitors either love or hate Pai. There's not much middle ground. Here you'll find plenty of hammocks strewn about, quick access to waterfalls, great and cheap eats, and beer that flows like water. Pai magically captured the beach vibe without the beach. Many expats live here part-time. Life is so laid back and simple that swinging in a hammock aligns with the intrinsic pace.

If you are looking for work, it's tough going in Pai, unless you work online.

Weather

Both CR and Pai are nestled in the northern mountains. This means the winters are cold. Temperatures drop to as low as 51 F, 10 C. You might think, "That's not bad." But remember, Thai houses are built to stay cool, not warm. Plus, I've never seen a heater in Thailand. Summers in Pai range from 88 - 99 F, 32- 37 C. CR is slightly cooler topping out at 93 F, 33 C. They both suffer from the smoke in the burning season (March - April).

What to Do

In Chiang Rai, expats lead a quiet and simple life. It's a great place to write that memoir you've always wanted to write. Pai is the contrast, because there's always someone to hang out with, dinners, drinks and chats to be had. The expat community is welcoming, be it for a few days or a few years. If you're looking for adrenaline-packed distractions, it will be hard to find them here.

Where to Live

CR doesn't have many housing options. You should hire or coax a Thai speaker, or real estate agent to assist you in your search for an apartment or house. The bang for your buck is huge in Chiang Rai! With just $125 you can score a large house with a surrounding garden.

Pai is packed full of cute little bungalows and houses. The downside is, most don't have kitchens. There are some family friendly houses around, however, they just require more searching.

TIP
Paying in advance for three months will work out much cheaper than the daily or monthly rate!

Proximity to Airport

Both Pai and CR have airports, Pai Airport (PYY) and Mae Fah Luang–Chiang Rai International Airport (CEI). But if you don't want to fly, take a bus from Chiang Mai (approximately 3 hours to Pai and Chiang Rai).

TIP
Both airports are served by small planes. It's something to consider if you are afraid of flying.

Social Requirements

Pai is all about socializing. If you're outgoing and open to new relationships, you'll have an awesome group of friends in no time at all! The expats scene in Chiang Rai is often comprised of retirees, expat's who are married to Thais, and retired school teachers. Expect a smaller social circle in CR, and pick this destination only if you are comfortable spending quality time by yourself or with your significant other.

THE EAST

Issan Region

Issan is the largest and poorest region of Thailand. Thais from Issan are stereotypically similar to hillbillies in North America. They have their own dialect of Thai (more similar to Lao language than Thai). Few expats start in Issan. Many expats married to Thais end up in Issan. The region is cheap, underdeveloped, mostly tourism-free and the indigenous nature is still intact. It may not be the perfect place to settle for an expat, but it's a great place to travel to see *authentic* Thailand.

Weather

Summers are hot in Issan. The highest average temperature here runs 90 F, the average low is 70 F, 70 C - 32 C. You could find yourself praying to the rain gods to bring in some relief. A main problem for expats in this region is the lack of air conditioned places to escape the heat. Of course, if you purchase or build here, you can fix said problem. That being said, good luck finding a repair man who knows how to fix an AC unit.

Many tourist destinations across the country have air-conditioned cafes, not Issan. In place of cafes, you might find yourself hanging out in 7-Eleven.

What to Do

If you enjoy gardening, motorbiking, exploring nature, or meeting friendly people, then this region is for you. There are less *farang* around so people will greet you everywhere you go. In the cities, there are shops and restaurants but the town is catered towards local comforts.

Where to Live

There are more accommodations and transportation options near the bigger cities of Khon Kaen, Udon Thani, and Ubon Ratchathani. Each of these cities boast decent transportation links to Bangkok and small expat communities. Housing options are simple, making a western-style kitchen a difficult find. Simple flats and large homes with gardens can be easily secured. Don't expect a turnkey house, you might need to put a bit of sweat and elbow grease into the house to make it comfortable.

Proximity to Airport

There are three major airports in Issan: Khon Kaen Airport (KKC), Ubon Ratchathani International Airport (UBP), and Udon Thani International Airport (UTH). All have regular flights to Bangkok and other domestic destinations. It's a breeze getting in and out of the Isaan region.

Social Requirements

The expat scene is almost non-existent, except for a few hot spots in the larger cities. There are foreigners living across the region but most enjoy the immersion into the Thai culture. They are often less friendly to expats because they're there for full immersion. Some basic Thai language skills are required here if you want to satisfy your basic needs with less stress. Central Thai dialect is quite different, so expect to learn some regional varieties. While the expats are often less than hospitable, the Thais are not! You'll make Thai friends quickly if you can speak some Thai.

THE GULF OF THAILAND ISLANDS

The islands are known for their beauty and their tourists! There are three islands (*Koh* in Thai) in particular that are full of expatriates, each with their own vibe.

Koh Samui

Koh Samui is the most upscale island in Thailand, boasting 5 star hotels, beautiful sandy beaches, and a European vibe (think Ibiza). The perfect place to live if you're hunting for affordable luxury. All goods are shipped in, being an island and all, so the price is higher than mainland Thailand. On the other hand, if you're earning a western wage or sitting on a comfortable pension, Koh Samui can grant you all the comforts you've grown accustomed to for less.

EXPAT EXPERIENCE

"Like many expats, we fell in love with Koh Samui after vacationing there. We decided we wanted to move to the tropics. Our first choice was Madagascar, since it was close to our home country, South Africa, so we could easily visit family. We traveled there a few times, but as our research deepened, we realized the education level wasn't up to par, and the medical facilities didn't suit our standards. We wanted our daughter to have the best education possible. Had it been just the two of us, we might have chosen this more 'adventurous and rustic' option. I didn't see myself home-schooling so we needed to find somewhere that ticked the boxes regarding lifestyle, education, and healthcare. Koh Samui did just that. Plus, we love the weather, feel extremely safe, and enjoy the friendly locals!"

~ Rosanne Turner, South African, Owner of www.samuitefl.com

Koh Phangan

Home of that pesky full moon party, often considered a right of passage for backpackers, is Koh Phangan. Every month, tourists flock to the island to drink too much and enjoy drunken company. A hedonistic place, half the island has been consumed by tourism, the other half by artists, modern yogis, spiritual seekers, and marijuana enthusiasts. Anything goes in Koh Phangan, and while it might seem like a crazy place, all of the expats I've met from there seem to be kind and gentle people. It's the perfect island if you want to explore a more alternative side to life.

EXPAT EXPERIENCE

*For six years, I lived on the north-west side of the island. It was a quiet
and serene place, as well as a hub for yogis, students, and spiritual new age healers. It
had classic beach bungalow accommodations . In fact, Srithanu as a whole, is full of
houses where people can rent long term and participate in hundreds of workshops and
courses that occur yearly. I own the Orion Healing Center, which is just one of the
many centers in the area, each with its own specialization. We specialize in
yoga, therapeutic juice fasting, and teaching healing modalities such as yoga. It's
extremely common to see people cycling with a yoga mat on their back to a class, or for
a great vegetarian lunch. Living in Koh Phangan is a truly beautiful experience for me.
It has a very slow pace, is quiet, and has easy access to anything one may need. Expats
with children take advantage of the primary school and the nursery. We just recently
moved to Samui with our two children in order to give them the 'best of both worlds'.
The tranquility of life on a Thai island as well as some western amenities, international
schools, and easy access to hospitals.*

~ Daliah, Orion Healing Centre, www.orionhealing.com

Koh Tao

If you love diving, this is the place to be. The underwater life is arguably the best in Thailand. If you don't dive or snorkel, then you might grow bored unless gazing into the water never tires. Many expats who seek employment work in either the diving or tourism sector of the island.

Koh Chaang

Koh Chang is the largest island in the southeast island cluster, close to the Cambodian border. The vibe here is quieter compared to other southern islands. Its' beauty draws its fair share of tourists during the Christmas and New Year holidays. Koh Chaang is the favorite get away spot for many expats. I've traveled to Koh Chaang four times in the last three years and would happily return tomorrow. There's a plethora of part-time expats living there who work online and want to enjoy the beach scenery as their "*office*." If you're lucky enough to visit during the off season, the Thais will happily welcome you since the island struggles to stay afloat without the revenue generated from tourism.

Weather

Island life can require you to endure monsoons. Monsoon season begins in October and lasts through December. The rest of the year, the islands boast blue skies and cool ocean breezes. The rainy season in the gulf islands is a bit different than mainland Thailand. Due to this, many folks flood the islands to avoid the rainy season on the mainland (June - September).

Things To Do

Water activities dominate island life, I know, you're shocked. In addition to splishy splashy events, there are yoga classes, boxing camps, Thai massage, forests to trek, and a healthy nightlife.

Accommodations

On Koh Tao, the cheapest island, there are accommodations ranging from simple guest houses to wooden huts on the beach. Koh Samui offers luxurious estates with sea views and plush modern condominiums. Koh Phangan has a mix of the above plus stand alone homes. The *hippy* bamboo bungalows are the most sought after. Guess that tells you a bit about the clientele on the island. While sleeping on the beach might not be your long-term plan, many have found themselves overnighting in the sand after a long full-moon party.

Proximity to Airport

Koh Samui has an airport with daily flights to Bangkok and a few other islands but tickets are costly. Koh Phangan is in the process of building an airport, so stay tuned. The most common method to access the Gulf is via the Surat Thani Airport (URT).[13] There's a high speed train from Bangkok that stops at Surat Thani Airport where you can transfer to a plane, ferry, or high speed boat. Connections run day and night.

Social Requirements

Personally, I've found the expats in the Gulf Islands to be friendly, outgoing, and extroverted. There are seemingly endless events and interesting people all around. Koh Samui is more business orientated comparatively. There you'll find more working expats than retired. That said, there are also numerous young expat families on Koh Samui, since there's a reputable international school.

EXPAT EXPERIENCE

"My favorite place to visit is Koh Wai. It's quiet, remote, and accommodations are pretty cheap. Most tourists and Thais have not discovered it yet. I usually go there at least once a year to relax and get away from Bangkok. One of my favorite memories was my first Songkran (New Years celebration) in Chiang Mai. I had never experienced it and being able to do so with close friends both foreigner and Thai was awesome."

~ Aaron

---

[13] http://www.suratthaniairport.com/

ANDAMAN COAST (SOUTHWEST)

If you've ever seen a picture of a Thai beach, chances are it was of either Krabi or Phuket. Many people don't realize they are both provinces, in addition to towns. It's the provinces that hold the sandy beaches, stunning karst mountains, and tropical party-filled islands. Known as both tourist and expat hubs for a reason. The Andaman Coast is home to jaw-dropping views! Many expats retreat here from Bangkok during the summer heat.

Phuket

Phuket is an island connected to the mainland by two bridges. It's also a tourist hub, packed with Swedish, Russian, and British tourists who've retreated from their winter (November - January). It's more developed and busy than Krabi. Patong Beach has a reputation akin to Pattaya. On the flip side, there's also family friendly beaches. Despite being an island, Phuket's easy access allows it all of the conveniences of the mainland. There's a booming property market, international schools, and hospitals who cater to the expat community.

EXPAT EXPERIENCE

"Phuket is the perfect mix of "East meets West." There's a vibrant cultural life with local markets, temples, and authentic villages, beautifully breathtaking beaches, modern malls and fancy restaurants as well as wild night life options. You can either live on a budget (eat with locals and shop in Thai markets) or eat in Western restaurants and hang-out with expats and tourists. My partner and I are able to live in a nice house, rent a new car and overall live a much better lifestyle than we would in any other European or American country. We both manage to save money from our salaries, while traveling on weekends and never worrying about money. We basically eat out every single meal and never think about how much we spend. We can even afford to hire someone to clean the house and do our laundry."

~ Julie Cousineau, primary school teacher

Krabi

Krabi is the laid-back, cool sister of Phuket. To the average eye, it looks like the typical Thai community, except it has it's own inhabited islands: Koh Lanta and Koh Jum. These islands offer some of the most relaxed island life in Thailand.

Koh Phi Phi is known for it's nightlife and stunning scenery. Expats that choose this area to settle in are some of the most chill beach-going people I've ever met. If you aren't a sun and sand worshipper, Krabi is probably better treated as a holiday rather than home.

Weather

Temperatures are reliably 82 - 97 F, 28 - 36 C, throughout the year. The challenge of the region is monsoon season (May -

November). Outside of the little old monsoons, Krabi and Phuket offer blue skies daily!

What to Do

The beach and the ocean are the biggest attractions in this coastal region. There are also mangroves, palm oil forest, island hopping, shopping, and beachside stalls to explore! Learn more about the Thai culture with a visit to the temples. After all of that exploration, sun, and sand, find a hammock and hangout! Life is carefree on the Andaman Coast!

Accommodations

Breath-taking views and a thriving tourism industry have driven up housing costs in Phuket and Krabi. Long-term (over a month) and low-season rentals will yield the best value. Quaint houses within a 10-20 minute drive to the beach can be found for

$760 a month. I would recommend you rent or own a motorbike or car for this location.

Proximity to Airport

Both Krabi and Phuket have international airports, Krabi Airport (KBV) and Puket International Airport (HKT). There are daily flights to Bangkok and Kuala Lumpur. Unfortunately, during high season, most international flights are chartered. Flights are often cheaper from neighboring Surat Thani, Trang, and Hat Yai airports. There are also cheap and easy bus connections to each airport option.

EXPAT EXPERIENCE

"A few years ago, I spent a weeklong holiday in Koh Lanta. I had a return flight to Chiang Mai from Hat Yai airport. I responsibly left ample time for the connection but did not anticipate that the ferry might break down. Wasn't the best of luck for me. After the initial panic, I called a bus company, and the owner desperately tried to find me a different flight. Murphy's law dictated that was the day all the flights were sold-out, so he ordered a minivan to pick me up and shuttle me STAT from Lantas port to the airport. It cost me $60 USD extra, but I made my flight!"

~ Laura Gibbs

Social Requirements

A laid back expat community awaits you in these provinces. Don't be offended if expats ask you endless questions, they're just friendly and love to be in the know. Gossip spreads like wildfire in these communities, so only share what you want to be shared.

DEEP SOUTH

The deep south has a troublesome reputation known for insurgency and occasional bombings. It's an area most expats opt to avoid. Neighboring Malaysia is easily accessed by train, making border runs by perpetual tourists a bit easier.

My experience as a tourist to the region was contrary to its reputation. I found it to have a relaxed pace with empty beaches. I felt safe traveling as a lone female, however, I recognize the area's safety can fluctuate quickly. While I didn't see many expats, I'm certain they must be hidden in the woodwork amongst beautiful little towns like Songkla. Hat Yai and Trang are the only sizable cities on the *farang* radar. Trang hosts boat tours to gorgeous islands such as Koh Lipe (read more below).

Hat Yai

Hat Yai is one of the largest cities in Thailand, and definitely the largest in the south, so there are plenty of amenities and things to do such as: endless shopping malls, restaurants, salons, supermarkets, food and clothes markets, bars, and clubs. Like most large cities, Hat Yai also has a shady side. Sadly, it's known as a sex tourism destination, thereby attracting some riffraff.

EXPAT EXPERIENCE

"In Hat Yai, the expat community is like a small town. We tend to know each other and frequent the same places. When I'm not teaching, I often meet my friends for dinner at a street food stall, small family-run restaurant, or one of the western pubs for a treat. There's a very nice Italian restaurant, German bar, and English pub. We mainly hang out at a sushi bar, or a bar run by Australians called The Hive. There's generally always someone around that I know, since we're a friendly community.

We also head to the park for picnics, sunbathe at Songkhla beach, or trek to the waterfalls. I love the zoo, especially since you can get close and interact with the animals. If we have a long weekend, my friends and I head to Ko Lipe or Krabi to enjoy an island vacation.

Although tensions are high at times, and bombings occur occasionally further south, I always feel safe here. That stuff never really affects Hat Yai. In guidebooks and the media, it seems like it is a dangerous place, but I have never experienced a fear for my safety or been affected by the bombings. There's always an army and police presence in the busiest areas, so I feel protected and believe the area is monitored well. I have spoken to loads of friends here who feel the same way. We were all apprehensive when placed here, but after we arrived, we realized that there was absolutely nothing to worry about. There's no conflict, or tension, that disrupts life in Hat Yai.

If you're looking to experience Thai city life, but you've already done Bangkok, Hat Yai is a great alternative before heading elsewhere in Asia. Another bonus is that it's close to many of the paradise islands. So if you're heading to the likes of Krabi, Ko Lipe, Ko Lanta, or Trang, there are flexible connections from there. We are also close to Malaysia, Singapore and other places so good for traveling around."

~ Sandy Dhaliwal, Geography teacher and freelance travel writer

---

Weather

The deep south is warm year-round 77 - 86 F (25 - 30 degrees C), and hosts monsoons and heavy rain from September through December. The wet season varies a bit depending on your location along the coast. The southwest islands tend to shutdown during the monsoons.

What to Do

The deep south offers easy access to numerous southern islands both large and small. You can island hop following a party route, or search for deserted beaches to sun worship. If nature is your vice, there are numerous outlets including gorgeous waterfalls. You can explore nearby Malaysia and its stunning islands, the Cameroon Highlands, or Penang. If you need a shopping fix, head to Hat Yai.

Accommodations

Typical accommodations include: guest house, condominium, concrete townhouse, and a detached house with a garden.

Proximity to Airport

Hat Yai International Airport (HDY) has domestic connections to Bangkok, Chiang Mai, Hua Hin, and Surat Thani (for the islands), as well as Singapore, and Kuala Lumpur. There's also a train-line that runs from Bangkok to Singapore, so getting to the major international airports is a synch.

Social Requirements

A little bit of Thai will go a long way down here (try to learn the southern accent). In larger cities or towns, there are expat communities to socialize with. Many *farang* in the deep south are a bit on the reserved side and are often married with a Thai family.

WEST

Kanchanaburi

Kanchanaburi, home to the *Bridge Over the River*, is an up and coming expat destination. It's also famous for its forests, mountains, caves, and waterfalls. Kanchanaburi is the country's third largest province, packed with evergreens but compared to its size, there are very few expats (now). If you want a quiet life near nature, Kanchanaburi could be ideal. The main city is small and manageable, and the tourism industry provides for the expat's basic needs – a supermarket, bar, bookshops and a steak house!

However, there are less job opportunities here. Much of the expat crowd are retirees and history lovers. Finding housing might be a little tricky (few expats stay more than a few months) and you'll probably need a Thai friend to help communicate, but you could always consider renting a guestroom by the river Kwai – long-term rates work out to be very cheap. Bangkok is also only an hour away if you need a big city break.

Mae Hong Son

Mae Hong Son is a quaint sleepy town nestled in the northwest corner of Thailand. It's one of my favorite places in Thailand, packed with nature! Life grudges along at a snail's pace here. There aren't many amenities for expats, but that's part of its charm. There are some Western restaurants and book-shops, but that's about it. In place of bars you have rolling mountains, waterfalls, and lots of French tourists. When you need more stimulation, Pai is just a three-hour bus ride away! Pai is a designated hippie town in a mountain valley. It's another place where expats end up lingering. Unless you work online or are a teacher, you aren't likely to find a job in Mae Hong son or Pai – both are more conducive to relaxation and enjoying the slower pace Thailand offers.

Mae Sot

Mae Sot is known as a grungy border town and home to much of the volunteer crowd. At first glance, the city holds little appeal but the longer you spend there, the more hidden gems you'll discover, literally, since Mae Sot is the Jade and Gold trading hub of the country.

Due to it's proximity, there is a prominent import/export business between Thailand and Myanmar here. There are also countless opportunities to volunteer and assist the numerous Burmese through refugee organizations strewn up along the border. The cost of living is modest, and great restaurants are plentiful!

Weather

Mae Sot's weather is less than ideal. *Winter* consists of two days where you can wear a jacket in the evening. The hot season is unbearable with daily temperatures reaching 100 F, 38 C. The rainy season is unmerciful for 2 or 3 weeks straight. Common inner dialog during this time of year include: *"Shall I go out? Nah, I'll wait 30 minutes until it stops pouring…"* [3 hours later] *"I'm so hungry! Screw it, where's my rain jacket?"* That being said, many expats acclimate well here.

What to Do

Volunteer. Your skill set, no matter what it is, can be useful to assist the Burmese refugees residing in Thailand. Teaching English is the most common volunteer activity. Simply approach any organization that you're interested in helping, and they will put you to work. The town is quiet (except in the bars), and is a great place to learn Thai or Burmese languages while living on the cheap.

If you're looking for some extra curricular sports, there are a couple of swimming pools and a *farang* mixed football team.

The mountains and surrounding forests beg an invitation

Accommodations

Accommodations are varied, but affordable across the board even when compared to the rest of Thailand. Simple studios, traditional wooden houses, gated villas, or newly built town-homes are all available to rent but can prove difficult to find at times. I suggest you drive the area you wish to live and ask the neighbors about any houses for rent or sale (read the *Try Before You Buy* section prior to purchasing a house).

Proximity to Airport

There's a domestic airport, Mae Sot Airport (MAQ), that serves the town with daily flights to/from Bangkok and soon connections to Yangon, Myanmar.

Social Requirements

The expat community is diverse, however, I'd say there are more 25-35 year old expats then pensioners here. Some expats have expressed that the clicks (groups of friends) can be hard to break into if you don't know anyone. With time, however, you should be adopted into a group. Since there is less to do here than in a big city, younger expats often create their own fun with themed parties, day trips, and pot luck dinners.

TRY BEFORE YOU BUY

Make sure to take time and weigh the benefits of renting property, at least initially, to the benefits of buying, even if the property is cheap. My advice is to live in Thailand at least six months, with a year being better, and explore this amazingly diverse country before you commit to purchasing.

Thailand's property market is impressive and expansive, ranging from high-rise studio apartments to hillside villas boasting stunning views. You can find your dream house at a fraction of the cost you'd pay at home.

Living in Thailand for at least a year helps you understand the market a bit better and the complications of foreign ownership. You'll also learn about the over supply of inventory to demand that could make selling a nightmare.

I'm British, the dream is to own property, much like it is for North Americans. The housing market in both the UK and North America is incredibly difficult for the younger generations or golden year goers. After seeing the bargain prices, like apartments going for $33,500, it's hard to resist. A simple search of property in Thailand will bring up hundreds of expat-run real estate companies.

TIP
Use caution when placing a Thai spouse's name on a deed. I've heard countless stories of the wife and her family claiming everything and ditching the estranged husband! The laws certainly favor the Thai in real estate matters.

If you want to buy, hire a good lawyer. Ask around or go through a reputable real estate agent (even if it costs a little extra). Foreign ownership is confusing. Expats can lease land or buy into a condo that is 51% Thai-owned. There are ways around the laws but the return on the investment might not be worth the hassle. What type of visa you have can complicate ownership even more.

If you want to rent, it's as easy as arriving and moving in, provided you have the cash for a deposit. As a rule, the more luxurious the place, the more hassle it is to rent. To rent a simple, comfortable condo, the process is two-fold: hand over the cash and sign an agreement. Most places ask for a three-month lease but will allow you to stay month to month at a higher rate (i.e. $216, for one month, versus $185 for 3 months). Renting is simple and affordable in Thailand.

Renting vs. Buying

Let's run down the pros of each route. Feel free to add your own values and priorities to the list.

RENTING

+ *Lots of options* — from budget rooms to luxury houses, and everything in-between

- *Affordable* — an average comfortable studio apartment costs between $100- $230 per month. A three bedroom house averages $400 - $500 per month.
- *Little paperwork* — You just need to show your passport and cash!
- *City hopping* — You can sample life in Thailand's different regions (If you are not tied to a job then you can avoid Thailand's bad weather - spend a Bangkok rainy season on Koi Samui, or Chiang Mai's burning season in the South)
- Ability to pick up and leave
- Moving away from a city's development problems. I used to rent a condo on a busy road in Chiang Mai. After battling rush hour traffic daily, noise at night, and a constant stream of tourists, I gave up and moved to a more quiet part of the city. The only difficulty I had moving apartments was finding a friend with a car to move my stuff
- Preview of a house you may purchase. If you are renting a property and love it then why not make an offer to the owner? Oftentimes, they are happy to negotiate a deal, making it a win-win for everyone

BUYING

- A beautiful home at a bargain price
- Numerous real estate agents, many of which are expats themselves and all will speak English
- A place to call home
- Ability to *customize* your abode (again at cheap prices)
- Easy to get *extension permits*
- A chance to gain equity if the value rises
- Potential rental income if you decide to rent the house (commonly done in Thailand among expats)

COST OF LIVING

Thailand fits all budgets: from barebones to five-star living

Foreign Currency	Baht per 1($€£) Currency
Dollar	30 Baht
Euro	40 Baht
Pound Sterling	50 Baht

   I'm going to start this section by showing you my budget for an average month. Keep in mind I'm a single young adult without kids. This will guide you to the lower end of the cost of living pendulum. Despite a seemingly low wage, it's adequate for a comfortable lifestyle and (outside Bangkok or the beaches) I rarely feel like I'm on a budget. For more information about jobs and wages in Thailand please read the **Work Hard Play Hard** section.

   Per month expenses and income:

Description	Income (USD)	Expense (USD)
English Teacher Chiang Mai	$1,000	
Rent /Studio Apt		$ 135
Utilities (water, electric, and wifi)		$ 23
Food (2 meals out daily, coffee, & drinks on the weekends)		$ 433
Toiletries		$ 20
Phone pre-paid sim		$ 20
Gas for Motorbike		$ 17
Motorbike rental		$ 93
Travel (overnight, once a month)		$ 75
Other (i.e. clothing, gifts, etc)		$ 100
Total		$ 923

My utilities are low because I rarely run air-conditioning (only in the hot season) — a fan is usually sufficient because I really enjoy steaming weather.

COUPLE

The following is a sample budget for a couple living in Bangkok:

✦Rent for a studio apartment: $350
✦Utilities (Water, Electric and Wifi): $100
✦Food (including 2 meals out daily, coffee and drinks on weekends): $500
✦Toiletries: $40
✦Phone credit pre-paid 3G and calls: $40
✦Transport (petrol/ public transport): $80
✦Motorbike rental: $100
✦Entertainment: $60
✦Travel (overnight, once a month): $100
✦Other (e.g. clothing, gifts, etc): $100

Average total expenditure for two = **$1,470 per month**

FAMILY

Here is a sample budget for a family of four living outside of Bangkok:

✦Rent for a townhouse/flat (outside of Bangkok): $600
✦Utilities (Water, Electric and Wifi): $215
✦Food (including 2 meals out daily, coffee and drinks on weekends): $500
✦Toiletries: $60
✦Phone credit pre-paid 3G and calls: $125
✦Transport (motorbike/car + petrol/ public transport): $200
✦Entertainment: $100
✦Travel (overnight, once a month): $300
✦Other (e.g. clothing, gifts, etc): Depends on family $150 +

Family of 4 total (outside Bangkok, not including school fees which can range from $400 - $18,500 per year) = **$2,250.**

That being said, I have spoken to many expat parents who claim their family of four lives easily on $1,550 monthly. A huge budget changer is school fees. The range is so large it could double your monthly budget if you chose one of the more expensive schools.

Let's dig deeper into each section to help you figure out your budget. I will share how much it cost for single folks and those with families. Housing, western food, and travel are usually the most expensive costs.

TIP

"School fees depend on the age and year-group of your child. The older the student, the more expensive it is. To give you a rough idea, at the time of writing, yearly fees for a student in Grade 6 or 7 range from $3,200 to $15,400 depending on the school. The bilingual schools are much cheaper as they're essentially Thai schools with some lessons taught in English. The bilingual schools follow the Thai academic calendar which is completely different from the Western academic calendar."

~ Alex Gunn, Author 'A year in Chiang Mai'

FOOD

Thai's love, which has lead to an international restaurant culture. There's a huge variety of food and expense. A meal at a local Thai restaurant with plastic chairs or a street stall will run around $1.00 -$1.20. While street food often comes with a bad stigma from other less-than-cleanly venders around the world, in Thailand it's delicious, has generous portion sizes, is occasionally spicy, and is safe to consume. Food poisoning by street vender is very rare here. Of course if it's date night or you'd like more ambiance, there are other restaurants that will accomplish those needs with an additional cost ($5 - $10 a plate).

If you eat at the previously mentioned local Thai restaurants three times a day for a month ($1.00 x 3 x 30days = $90) and indulge in a coffee or fruit smoothie every day ($1.00 x 30 days = $30), you would have spent $120. To put that into perspective, if I bought a large mocha from Starbucks each morning in the United States, my monthly Starbucks expense would be ($4.96 x 30) $148.80, over $28 bucks more than my entire food expense in Thailand if I ate out three times a day and had a daily fancy coffee!

Tourist areas and foreign cuisine are more expensive than a normal Thai restaurant. As a rule, it'll be double or triple the price. However, even at double the price, eating out is still very affordable. Bangkok is as expensive as Thailand gets. Prices start at $1.54 for street food but climb to $30 - $40 at 5-star restaurants which is still a great value when compared to other countries. To give you an idea about the variance of expense per region see the examples below.

Town	Green Curry & Rice	Coffee
Bangkok	$5.00 - $10.00	$ 3.50
Beach	$2.50 - $5.00	$ 2.50
Thai City	$1.00 - $5.00	$ 1.50

LOCAL MARKETS

Thailand's local markets are amazing. They offer fresh local vegetables, fruit, and spices by the kilo. Large American-styled supermarkets are found in all large towns, but I would recommend the local market to buy produce. The produce is fresher, local, and much cheaper than in the large supers. In some expat hubs, international supermarkets have popped up since demand for imported foods has increased. These markets give you many of the products you miss from home, but you'll pay dearly for them. They also offer a wide variety of bread, cheese, drinks, chocolate, sweets, condiments, biscuits, etc. While many of the products are more expensive, some are equivalent, like peanut butter.

WATER + ALCOHOL

A few cents of your budget will have to go towards water. Tap water is not drinkable. Bottled water is available everywhere but an even cheaper, and eco-friendly solution is reverse-osmosis water machines which charge just $.03 a liter.

If you're a social drinker, a large beer will run you around $1.50 from a shop and at a bar will run around $3.00. Thai whiskey brands are super cheap. A small bottle of SangSom whiskey is just $4.00. Wine is more expensive since it's not produced in Thailand. A glass of wine at a restaurant averages around $3.00 - $6.00.

HOUSING

The availability and affordability of housing is immense. From basic, grungy studio ($77 per month), bachelor pad ($430), town house ($770) or even luxury villa estate with sea views ($3,080) you can save money on accommodations or live in the house you've always dreamt about. Inventory for both houses and condos are high.

If you plan to stay somewhere for more than 6 months, you can get a discounted price. However, renting short-term allows you more freedom to move around and explore different areas of Thailand.

If you opt to purchase a home, you will have to pay a transfer fee (2%) and stamp duty (0.5%), however, you can negotiate for the seller to pay the fees.

UTILITIES

Utilities are refreshingly affordable. Water is only $.46 per unit. Depending on the size of your place, it can be as cheap as $5

- $10 (Studio - House). Electric is just $0.25 per unit, resulting in expenses not much more than water! If you're a large family who runs the dryer and AC a lot, expect to see a much higher bill. Electricity prices are standard across most of Thailand, Bangkok being an exception as they charge a premium rate.

If you're planning on renting, you can usually negotiate utilities into your rent. It's nice for your peace of mind, not having to keep tabs on the different bills. Air-conditioning easily doubles your electric bill. It's a good idea to visit potential homes during the daytime to see if they are shaded or hot and need air-conditioning. It's also advisable to cruise the streets at night to see if the neighborhood is loud. Internet with wifi starts at $9.25 for a simple connection. Faster speeds are available for an additional cost.

FEES

Transferring money or withdrawing cash from an ATM usually results in a small fee. Those fees, while minimal, add up over time. My first three months living abroad cost me over $260 in currency transaction and ATM fees. That lesson lead me to a new bank that didn't charge ATM fees or currency transaction fees. Read the *Banking* section to learn how you can avoid fees.

Until recently, one ATM offered free withdrawals (opposed to the $4.63 fee). Foreigners would drive 15 minutes to the remote ATM to avoid the fee. If you have a work permit, you can open up a bank account for free. Otherwise, there's a one-time fee for the cash card ($9.25) to open a savings account on a tourist visa. Loans in your name are extremely difficult to secure so most expats purchase with cash or loans from their home countries.

TRANSPORTATION

For many expats on a budget, it makes more financial sense to buy a motorbike (see the **After You Arrive** section for more information). Renting a small automatic bike runs around $93 per month plus petrol. Otherwise, you can take *songthaews* everywhere at $0.62. In Bangkok, a mixture of Skytrain, Metro, and taxis average $123 - $150 a month if you work or travel within the city often. If you have the time to spare, the BKK bus is only $0.31 a journey and is a great way to see the city.

To register a motorbike in your name, you'll pay between $6 - 25 (depending on the model and age of the bike). You should get a 'green book' when you buy your bike which has the names of previous owners. You also have to pay insurance annually and tax.

The cost of diesel is around $1.24 per liter, 91 Gasohol is $1.11 per liter (roughly $4.20 per gallon). Most motorbikes use gasohol and their tanks hold about 2 liters.

VEHICLE EXPENSES

Motorbikes are the most economic vehicle option in Thailand. Learning how to drive is fairly straightforward, however, I would recommend taking a safety course and securing your motorcycle endorsement prior to arriving when possible.

A decent used automatic scooter will set you back $550 - $925 depending on the condition. A new scoot is about $1388. Larger motorcycles are also available, but I recommend renting them first to decide if it suits your needs. Renting a scooter will cost around $93 per month. After six months you would have spent enough to buy one. Check websites like Craigslist and Facebook's 'buy and sell' groups to find second hand deals.

Scooters aren't for everyone. Purchasing a car is also affordable and convenient, especially in the wet season. A used car will run around $3700 -$6200 whereas new cars start at $10,795 - $12,300.

When you purchase a car, you'll be given a blue book to register the car. Registration will run around $12 - 30, insurance is $8, and tax runs about $7.

REPAIRS

New cars and motorbikes come with a one or two year warranty for repairs at their corresponding dealerships. Otherwise, mechanics can be found across the country. If you get a flat tire, you're never more than five minutes away from a mechanic, although you might not realize it. Sometimes the nearest shop is the house down the hill. Mechanics charge very little for labor, and most of the parts are cheap. I replaced a battery in my scooter for $25. Not all mechanics speak English, so be prepared for a game of charades.

DOMESTIC HELP

It's quite easy to find a maid, although you'll need to ask around to find a good one. Having your house cleaned starts at $3.00 for an apartment, and around $12 for a house. A live in maid, who often also doubles as a babysitter, will run about $615 a month. Maids are usually Burmese, Lao, or Cambodian.

Laundry is a separate issue. You could pay your maid to do laundry but Thailand is full of laundry shops (it's strange how many there are). You can hand a bag of dirty laundry to the shop and collect it cleaned, dried, and ironed a day later! Laundry costs about $0.93 per Kg. If your house doesn't have a washer and dryer and you'd prefer to launder your clothes yourself, head to a nearby laundry mat and drop $0.30-0.60 into each machine.

MEDICAL COSTS

In the **Healthcare** section, I will go into greater detail, but for now I'll provide a general overview. Doctors visits, hospital stays, prescription medicine, and dental work are much more affordable here than North America. If you shop around, you can find western qualified doctors at a fraction of the cost. In the past, dental work was a bargain but prices have been steadily rising. The cost of a complex filling set me back about $123, recently. Most cities have at least two hospitals: a private, ritzier hospital and a cheaper, government-run hospital that is often prone to longer wait times.

As for medicine, it's the same structure either the cheap generic Thai brand or the more expensive name-brand version. For example, one generic antibiotic is $2.78 the name-brand version of said antibiotics runs $7.82; getting cured, priceless.

TRAVEL

Travel should be factored into your budget because I doubt you traveled across the world to your new home without plans to explore your new country or surrounding Asia. I've got great news, you don't have to save much to explore much. A weekend getaway can cost as little as $34 including a guest house. With more comfortable accommodations, you still won't break $100 for a weekend.

Travel transportation is one of the few costs that don't vary greatly throughout the country. A ten hour journey on a government bus starts at $13 with VIP service running just $30. Domestic flights start at just $20. Many expats watch for these steals and book well in advance, since it's so cheap it doesn't matter if you cancel later. There's a pleasant train network that allows you to see much of the country, however, they're likely to experience delays. The local train from Bangkok to Hat Yai is under $3 but it's cramped and takes a long time to get anywhere. Taking it is more of a cultural experience than efficient means of transportation.

1ST MONTH'S BUDGET

During the first few months living in Thailand, your budget will be higher than usual. You won't know where the cheapest good eats are, or how to haggle in Thai. You might also encounter overpriced accommodations because you were making reservations online and were charged the Americanized pricing prior to your arrival.

PHONE

Many people use Line, Whatsapp (messaging apps), Facebook, and Skype to keep in contact with loved ones around the world. Calls and messages are cheap and pre-paid sims can be purchased at 7-Elevens for $9.25. For just $12 you can score unlimited data on your smart phone. In Bangkok, there is fast 4G service and most other major cities have reliable 3G service. See the *Communication* section in *After You Have Arrived* for more information.

TRANSPORT

I don't recommend renting a motorbike in Bangkok, the traffic is intense. It's hard enough to navigate with a car. Most other regions are manageable for a new *moto* driver. The cheapest and healthiest mode of transportation is your own two feet or a bicycle. You can buy one for just $60 USD. Many cities across the country are bike friendly. Just remember, it's hot here, so you'll sweat up a storm.

It's a great luxury to have a car, and many expats decide that's the best option for them. Air conditioning, a roof (for when it rains), cruise control, and the freedom to explore the country at your leisure, are all amazing benefits afforded to a car owner!

BEFORE YOU ARRIVE

LOGISTICS

My father has a long checklist consisting of everything one needs while on a holiday. It's two pages and ranges from your toothbrush, foreign currency, and underwear, to emergency biscuits and cheese *(sounds strange but the cheese was useful in India)*. While his list is a useful tool for most countries, it was somewhat irrelevant when it came to Thailand.

On my plane to Thailand, I chit-chatted with the man seated next to me. He was traveling with just a small bag for an entire month. He talked too much to be a minimalist, so I asked him why he didn't bring more luggage. He explained that he visits Thailand every year and has learned that he can buy what he needs along the way. "Why carry deodorant and shampoo half way across the world when you can buy it in 7-Eleven for cheaper?" This was the opposite side of the pendulum from my father's protocol, but for Thailand it made sense. In fact, when my father came to visit me, he ended up leaving half his suitcase here in order to fill it with beautiful, useful, and cheap Thai goods to take home.

The take home message here is this section is designed to help you move easier and lighter. You don't need to pack the kitchen sink, or emergency cheese, but there are some things you might want to buy or do before you make your way to *the land of smiles*.

SORTING OUT DEBT

Thailand can be a great place to pay off debts while living well, but not a place to make serious money, unless you're earning an international paycheck. Upping and moving here can be as cheap as the plane ticket. The cost of living is low which means *becoming an expat* in Thailand is possible even if you have student loans or credit card debt. That being said you always have more options and are more free the lower your monthly overhead. If an international life is what you seek, work towards eliminating debt.

If you have a loan, talk to your bank before you leave. Set up a direct debit from the appropriate account in order to pay off the loan, or ask what they recommend for international payment. A friend of mine pays his school loans once every two months to halve the international transfer fee. Another expat pays their loan from their bank at home and uses their Thai wages to fund their Thai-accrued expenses. Read more about how to save on international fees and setting up the best international banking situation in the **Money Matters** section.

If you don't have any debts, congratulations! You're in an excellent position to take full advantage of the affordability in Thailand!

EMERGENCY FUND

Time and time again I hear the fear, "What if I run out of money and am stuck here?" With proper planning, that should never happen. No matter what country or city you live in, you should save up a minimum of three months living expenses. That way, you'll have an adequate amount of time to regroup and change financial strategies if needed. Also, plan on bringing a little extra cash upfront for the deposit for your accommodations, your visa, and transportation.

TIP
Eating Thai food often, and learning to curb your pizza cravings will save you a lot of coin.

A great way to earn your emergency fund or help cancel your debt while prepping your move is by selling your car, renting your house out (if you own), and sell most of your belongings on E-bay and Craigslist. Read more about what to do with your stuff in the *Logistics* section.

SECURE DOCUMENTS

After reading the Immigration section, you should have an idea about what documents you'll be required to furnish and have notarized. Make sure to have a few copies of your bank account statements and all other documents (to show Thai immigration you can afford your life in Thailand). Chase down your docs early so your new life is not held up by paperwork.

If you plan to work in Thailand, make sure you have copies of your school degree, transcripts, letters of recommendation, and any other paperwork that would be pertinent for an interview.

Bring copies of your immunization and medical records. If you have a living will, make sure you have a copy with you. I recommend scanning and saving all important documents on your computer and on a cloud service like Dropbox, Onedrive, or Googledrive. For those of you who aren't familiar with cloud services, it's simply a back up of your information that is redundantly stored off-site. You can upload a document to your account at www.dropbox.com (or other cloud provider) and it's saved to one of their thousands of servers around the world. That way, if your computer crashes and you can't locate a paper copy, you can log into any computer around the world and pull up the document. Read more about how to use electronics to facilitate your expat life in the *Gadgets & Communication* sections.

Ensure your passport isn't going to expire soon and check how many pages you have left. A Thai visa usually takes up a whole page and visas to nearby countries also require space. It might not seem important now but lack of space creeps up on many people. When renewing your passport, you can ask for extra pages. Once in Thailand, you can have extra pages sewn into American passports (but not European passports). If you have kids, make sure you apply for their, passports well before your departure date.

Check if your drivers license is set to expire soon. If you don't have one, or your license expires while you're in Thailand, you can apply for a Thai license quite easily. Oftentimes you're not asked to show your license when renting scooters, instead they keep your passport as a deposit. I would still recommend that you follow all laws and maintain your license.

FOUR-LEGGED FRIENDS

If you consider your pet to be a part of the family, leaving him or her behind is not an option. Luckily, bringing animals into the Kingdom is not that tricky. When you're shopping around for the best airfare deals, make sure to also consider the best pet transportation deals. Some airlines don't allow snub-nosed animals (like pugs) as they might have difficulties breathing. They actually have problems in hot weather too, so think twice about bringing certain breeds to Thailand. Other airlines allow pets as a carry-on as long as they meet weight and space regulations. Your pooch or kitty needs to meet the following requirements:

✦ Been a resident in its home country for at least 6 months
✦ Has an export certificate from his/her home country
✦ Secure an identity and health certificate
✦Show proof of vaccinations and certificates against Rabies, Leptospirosis, Distemper, Hepatitis and Parvovirus (**21 days before departure**)
✦ Cats also need Feline Enteritis and Feline Flu vaccinations

Once your furry friend arrives in Thailand, you'll need to grab an import permit from the animal import desk. *Be prepared to pay a "fee"*. If the "fee" sounds too steep, give a counter offer with a smile. Getting angry with Thai officials will only cause you problems, so stay calm and smile. If the animal is coming from a rabies-free country (like Costa Rica), then they won't need to be quarantined.

EXPAT EXPERIENCE

"Importing a dog from the USA wasn't too much trouble for us. We researched online and were aware that there might be a bribe of as much as $100 to get the dog in. With our Medical Certificate and Vaccinations in hand, we boarded the airplane with our dog stowed under our seat. After what felt like an eternity, we arrived in Thailand. Somehow they knew we were coming (airline told them?), and they pulled me into an office. $3, and many copies later, we were out of the office. I was shown that importing an elephant would have cost me around $8. No clue if the numbers were a bribe or not. You never know in Thailand. It was harder to export Dillon, our dog, out of Thailand. It required the same Medical Certificate (standard for any pet traveling anywhere) and an export license. We ended up shipping our dog using a cargo company to get him out of Thailand. Travel within Thailand technically requires a permit though we ignored those rules."

~ Nicolas, Vicky, and Dillon the dog

PET POLICIES BY AIRLINE

United:	American:
http://bit.ly/unitedpetpolicy	http://bit.ly/americanpetpolicy
Delta:	Asiana
http://bit.ly/deltapetpolicy	http://bit.ly/asianapet
Finnair	Korean
http://bit.ly/finnairpet	http://bit.ly/koreanpet
Emirates	Etihad
http://bit.ly/emiratespet	http://bit.ly/etihadpet

Lufthansa	Air China
http://bit.ly/lufthansapet	http://bit.ly/airchinapet
Japan Airlines	Singapore
http://bit.ly/japanpet	http://bit.ly/singaporpet
Cathay Pacific	Qatar Airways
http://bit.ly/cathaypet	http://bit.ly/qatarpet

ONLINE RESOURCE

Thailand Pet Regulations - US,[14] Canada[15], Anglioinfo

MAIL SYSTEM

The ideal mail system either utilizes a loved one at home who receives and opens mail for you, or an international mail company that will scan all of your mail allowing you to decide what gets shipped onward to Thailand and what gets shredded. My mum takes care of my mail and emails me when she thinks something is important.

Secondly, make as many things paperless as possible. Set your bills and notifications to electronic delivery and cancel your paper subscriptions.

Create a list of everyone that might need to be informed about your address change. Start the process early, you would be

---

14http://moacdc.thaiembdc.org/htmls/faq.html

[15] http://www.thaicongenvancouver.org/cms/index.php?option=content&task=view&id=139

surprised how the list will grow over time. Conversely, try to remove your name and address from as much mail as possible. Unsubscribe from magazines, catalogues, and other mailers you receive.

If you don't want your helpful family member to read your mail, or you don't want to ask for such a large favor, then sign up for a mail service such as Jetbox[16] Atlas International Mail,[17]or International Mail Service .[18] They'll provide you with a US address. The mail they receive will be scanned, then a notification emailed will be sent to you. From there, you decide what you want them to do with the mail. Some companies use an app so you can manage everything from your smart phone.

BANKING

Thailand has numerous large bank chains distinguished mostly by color. Their services and protections are fairly equivalent across the board. I noticed many Thai's don't use banks. I'm not sure if that's because of poverty, tradition, or distrust.

Many expats opt to keep their money in banks in their home country, only utilizing Thai banks in order to withdraw funds. This works well if your bank doesn't charge ATM fees. Take a look at your bank and see if they will suit you as an international bank. Test your bank with the following questions. Does my bank allow me to:

✦Withdraw money internationally without fees
✦Exchange currency without a fee

---

[16] http://bit.ly/jetbox

[17] http://bit.ly/Atlasmail

[18] http://bit.ly/internationalmail

✦Connect with online banking and telephone banking (for emergencies)
✦Transfer money to foreign accounts
✦Accept direct debits and automatic deposits (for pension, social security, rental income from your house, etc.)
✦Recoup lost money through insurance if it is stolen (hacked)

There are three potential international charges you need to look out for when accessing your money abroad.

Foreign Transaction Fee (FTF)– applied by Visa/MasterCard to complete an international transaction. In theory, it's applied to cover the risk of fraud from foreign transactions. Most cards average 0.8% of the transaction. This fee is more common to credit cards but banks often charge the fee as well. There are many credit cards that do not charge this fee (Sapphire Preferred and Venture One for example). Most UK banks don't charge a foreign transaction fee. Charles Schwab also does not charge a FTF.

Currency Exchange Fee (CEF)– Each time you withdraw a currency different from the currency in your bank, you can be hit with a currency exchange fee. You can also be charged a CEF when using your bank card out and about if the bill is in a currency other than your bank account's currency. Additionally, see what exchange rate your bank is providing. Charles Schwab does not charge a CEF.

ATM Fee – Often, you will get hit with this fee from both ends. Your bank will charge for using an out of network bank, and the out of network bank will charge for accessing their bank's funds. Thai banks usually charge $4.50 - $5.50. Charles Schwab not only does not charge a fee for using an out of network ATM, they refund you the fee that other banks impose!

TIP

Usually the best exchange rate occurs by withdrawing from the ATM. If you are hit with ATM fees, however, you lose your potential savings. The maximum withdrawal amount per transaction through an ATM is $300. If you need more, head inside the bank and use a teller.

Prior to departure, make sure and tell your bank that you will be withdrawing money from Thailand. I also recommend having a credit card or two as back ups in case your account gets blocked due to an early fraud warning or "suspicious activity." I've had my card blocked a few times. While it's inconvenient to call the bank to unblock it, I'm still happy they're safeguarding my money.

There are ATMs all over Thailand (one is attached to each 7-Eleven). Their withdrawal rates are fairly the same across the board, but if you have an account with Charles Schwab, it wouldn't matter! If you plan to travel to small villages or rural areas, bring enough cash to cover the duration of your stay.

Many tourist areas have foreign currency exchange centers that offer reasonable rates and are commission free. So you can come to Thailand with dollars and exchange once you're here. Neighboring countries accept dollars for visa entry fees (Baht not accepted) so keep a small supply ($10 and $20 notes) for when you travel across the border.

I arrived in Thailand with travelers checks thinking it was the safest and best option. While the banks can exchange them, I had to pay a bank and processing fee and fill out a million forms. In hindsight, they weren't worth the hassle.

CREDIT CARDS

Cash is the only method of payment for many stores and restaurants across the country. Credit cards are only accepted in major hotels and international chain stores. That said, you should have a credit card in order to access and withdraw emergency money from home. You can withdraw money with your credit card from bank tellers.

Evaluate your current credit card. Does it serve you and your goals? If you're a big traveler, find a card that rewards you with travel benefits. If you're not into travel but would like a percentage rebate on spending, get the card that offers the best rebate program. I met one expat who got air miles that equalled a free international flight just for signing up for that card and spending $500 with them (he bought his wife's flight on the card). Most major airlines have their own rewards credit card. Decide which frequent flier program will work best for you (flies where you want to travel) and figure out how best to work their frequent flier and credit card rewards points.

Chase Sapphire Preferred[19] card offers great points (40,000 points was the offer at the writing of this book) for signing up and spending $3000 USD in the first three months (that's enough for a one way ticket to Thailand from North America. All you'd have left to pay are taxes which can be as low at $20 USD). You can use the points to redeem flights on BA, Korean air, and United. Thai Airways has an American Express card[20] that let you accrue points towards free flights, upgrades, flight discounts, and 50% off companion tickets. Keep an eye out for the upcoming book *Becoming a Nomad* to learn more about how to work the airline miles system to your benefit, travel for a living, and for more travel & life hacks.

---

[19] http://bit.ly/chasesapp

[20] http://bit.ly/ThaiAmex

PAYPAL

Another great way to transfer money is through <u>Paypal</u>. Link your bank account to your Paypal for the most versatility. You can buy online with your Paypal account, send money to and receive money from friends, and bill clients for services.

TIP
Thai coins and bills bear His Majesty's face on it, so handle the money with care. *Never step on a coin that's rolling away* or a note in the wind. You will get angry looks and could even be arrested under the lèse majesté law which prohibits disrespectful acts or behavior towards the King and Royal Family!

YOUR STUFF

Ever heard the saying, *"The stuff you own ends up owning you"*? Throughout your preparations to move abroad, your appreciation for the saying will grow immensely. Less is usually more. This section is designed to teach you what to bring to Thailand, what you can buy here, and what to ditch!

The first step is to take stock of what you have and what you use on a regular basis. I know expats who live on a beautiful beach who are mentally still sorting through their stuff at home because they stored everything and didn't sort through and make hard decisions before leaving.

Start sorting your stuff today. Pick a room and get to it. Leave the kitchen for last. Create bags designated for: donation, Thailand, and undecided. Conquer a room a week. The following week, return to the room just completed and review the contents in the undecided bag. Make a final decision about its contents and stick to it. If you haven't used it in the last six months, you don't need it.

Imagine your life in Thailand. How does your house look? The clearer the picture, the better idea you'll have of what you need. Do you imagine a simple white condo with sea views? Do you also see two DVD players, an exercise ball and 50 romance books? Less is more!

STARTING FRESH- *the pro purging argument*

It's cheap to furnish and decorate a home in Thailand. Plus, you can sell your stuff on eBay, Craigslist, or Gumtree adding to your relocation funds. This is a great project to enlist a tech savvy, financially motivated family member to assist you. Offering them 10 - 20 percent of the profits can result in a motivated A-team. Conversely, if you decide to rent your house, you can keep your furnishings and rent it furnished. In my experience, a furnished rental rents for at least an extra hundred dollars a month.

Shipping your house-full of goods is expensive and time consuming. Oftentimes, the items you use on a daily basis can fit into a few suitcases. Walking to your gate knowing that everything you own is on the plane with you is a liberating experience. New life, new beginnings, new stuff!

EXPAT EXPERIENCE

"We arrived with a backpack, a mini-stereo, and my favorite pillow! Before leaving South Africa, we sold whatever didn't have sentimental value and stored the rest with family. Each year we visit family in South Africa. We return to Thailand with a few items we decided we wanted in Thailand each trip. It's possible to purchase almost everything you need once here, but it's no longer cheaper than South Africa. Bedding is much more expensive here. I miss good quality leather shoes! I do a major shop for essentials when at home."

~ Justine Bristow, South African, Kindergarten Head teacher

WHAT TO BRING

CLOTHES

The average Thai body is a fraction of the size of an American, Canadian, or European. The larger cities sell international brands with a large range of sizes, however the smaller towns or markets stock *Thai-sizes*. It always pains me when I can't fit into the largest size. I'm US 6-8 and the average Thai waist is 0-1. I'm also tall so shopping for trousers here is difficult, which is why I often end up wearing skirts. Another solution is to have clothes custom made for you. It's cheap and easy so keep this option in mind if you need a special suit or dress.

Make sure to pack plenty of lightweight summer clothing: shorts, jeans, hat(s), swimming suits, flip flops, hiking shoes, t-shirts, and a lightweight jacket.

TIP
In the rainy / monsoon season, many houses are prone to mold. Books and folded clothes are the first things to be hit. Mold can be avoided by running the air conditioner or buying a dehumidifier. If you're behind in the battle and you have mold to kill, good ole' vinegar does an excellent job (better than bleach).

TOILETRIES

If you have a favorite face cream, mascara, aftershave, or other hygiene products bring it in bulk. Tampons and condoms can be bought here but if you are fussy about brand comfort then stock up. Of course, Thailand does sell hygiene products, but most likely not what you are accustomed to, and many complain that their brands pale in comparison.

UNDERWEAR

You'll run into the same size issues here. Once, I tried on Thai underwear that was too small to fit over my thigh. I no longer shop at the markets because it's destroying my body image! While you don't need to go crazy and pack a 100 pairs of undergarments, I do recommend you plan to visit Bangkok or an other larger city a couple of times a year to replenish your clothing needs. Ladies, bras are even harder to find, especially if you have a large cup size. Larger sizes will most likely have to be purchased online.

SHOES

Thailand has a great variety of women's shoes up to size 39, (women's 8). After that, your options drop off. I went to every shoe shop in Bangkok and Chiang Mai just to find something in size 40/41 (women's 9). Men's sizing is a bit better with sizes up to 44/45 (men's 10.5). If you find your larger shoe size, it's often too narrow. Stock up on a few pairs of waterproof shoes and summer sandals.

VITAMINS

If you have a specific vitamin or supplement regimen, bring a healthy supply of them. Basic multivitamins and vitamin C is easily purchased here, however, complex supplements are hard to find and expensive to import. Thailand does sell numerous herbal remedies.

COMFORT ITEMS

What can't you live without? Some expats opt to bring their favorite tea, liquor, or savory snack-food. For others, it's all about their soft blanket, t-shirt, or other cuddle-friendly object. Bring a few photos of family and friends to personalize your house and make it feel like your home.

ELECTRONICS

As a rule, electronics are cheaper in the States. Most expats arrive with a laptop and an unlocked smartphone. That should be sufficient unless your work involves special equipment, or you're a *"gear-head"* (if you don't know what that means, you're not one). If you want to buy a DSLR camera[21] to document your new exotic surroundings, get it in your home country. If a cheap point and click will suffice, buy it in Thailand. The price is the same and you wouldn't have to pack it.

There's a big electronics market in Thailand, especially for second hand stuff. So unless you want something specific like an Apple product, you can often find it second hand or new if you head to Bangkok.

Importing electronics after your move can be expensive due to hefty import taxes. If family or friends are planning a visit, ship them your new guilty pleasure, and they can bring it in their carry-on. Electronics are big targets for import duties, so I recommend carrying them on the plane. Older desktop computers can usually be shipped without a problem, but if it looks remotely new you may be paying for it, again.

RECOMMENDED ELECTRONICS include:

✦ Laptop
✦ Unlocked smart phone (you can opt to purchase this in Thailand)

---

[21] This camera has served me well if you're looking for an easy to use high quality DSLR: http://bit.ly/dslrnikon

- iPad / tablet (to use as an electronic reader or laptop replacement during travel)
- External hard drive[22] to back up those precious photos.
- USB /flash drive (to take documents to the printer or share films with friends)
- Waterproof phone case,[23] the Thai brands don't seem reliable.
- Camera if you want to have something better than the camera on your phone.
- Kindle or eReader, there are lots of second hand book shops but if you're after a new title, it's easier to buy it online.
- Mobile speakers[24]
- Videocamera and waterproof camera[25] with extra batteries. What good is a camera if the battery is dead?
- 140W adapter[26] for your car. Plug your computer, cell phone, air mattress pump, or anything else you'd like to use while on long road trips.

TIP

If you're having trouble locating an item, electronic or otherwise, show the clerk a picture of the item or the web page where it's sold. Usually the clerk can direct you to it in-store or the nearest store that sells said item.

American plugs will fit into Thai electrical sockets, however, you need to be mindful of the voltage your device can receive. Thai outlets are 240-volt, double the US voltage, so make sure

---

[22] bit.ly/lacie1T

[23] bit.ly/lfeprof

[24] bit.ly/h20speakers

[25] This video camera is best for rugged outdoor adventures: http://bit.ly/goproexpat

[26] This is the one I have: http://bit.ly/140Wadapter

your device can scale up (by reading the box at the end of the cord). Even if your devices are set up for higher voltage I still recommend that you pick up a travel adapter[27] so you won't run into problems when traveling to surrounding countries.

SHIPPING YOUR STUFF

I know far more people who have opted to start fresh than those who opt to ship a container. However, with a non-immigrant visa, you are entitled to import used personal effects[28] (furniture, carpets, books, musical instruments, paintings, tableware, stereos, linens, and similar household furnishings) tax/duty free. Items must have been **used** by the expat prior to shipping.

Shipping to Thailand can be a disaster if you don't know the rules.

"In cases where the household effects are electrical appliances e.g. radios, televisions, refrigerators, microwaves, ovens, air conditioners, etc., only ONE unit each of such items is eligible for tax and duty free allowance… Any excess unit shall be subject to regular taxes and duties, and Customs will place the items that have the lowest rate of duty under tax and duty exemption. It is important that the used/secondhand household effects must be imported not earlier than one month before or not later than six months after the arrival of the importers. Under exceptional circumstances, Customs may extend the time limits for the importers." ~ Thai customs http://bit.ly/thaiimportstuff

Thailand has high import taxes especially on electronics, so if you plan to import, make sure you time it right and have the correct visa (not a tourist visa). The official import information can be found on the Thai Customs website www.customs.go.th. Once on the website click the American flag in the top right corner to translate to English.

---

[27] This is the adapter I use, and as of the writing of the book it was just $3 http://bit.ly/worldelectric

[28]http://bit.ly/thaiimportstuff

EXPAT EXPERIENCE

"I decided not to pay the $25 per kilo excess luggage fee to the airline after a visit home. Instead I couriered it. Customs charged me import duty on all my clothes, even though I had bought most of my clothes in Thailand! Thai customs said "You should have registered the items leaving Thailand."

~ Anonymous

Any company can ship your stuff here but the right company can set you up for a successful and duty free experience. I highly recommend you pay a a little more upfront for door to door service rather than haggle and pay an unknown amount to retrieve your belongings from port.

EXPAT EXPERIENCE

"We shipped stuff from the UK. We hired a local company who specialized in international removals. It was all fine until it ended up in Bangkok. We got an email from a senior staff member there explaining if we wanted our stuff, we would have to pay "tea money". We were given a choice: pay a lot of money and get a receipt, or pay not so much and no receipt. We opted for 'not so much' and the following week a truck arrived with all our stuff. We were told that each day it was stored in port, we would be charged."

~ Alex Gunn, Author of, *A year in Chiang Mai*

Don't know where to start? Get an idea of the going rate by requesting a door to door quote through an aggregator like www.intlmovers.com. This website allows you to request multiple door to door quotes. If you find a company you like, ask them for a reference. After researching who most expats have used and are happy with, two names came up time and time again. Both offer door to door service.

EXPAT EXPERIENCE

While collecting a shipment at the port, one expat was explained there was a "fee" of $625 to release his stuff. He returned a few days later with a Thai friend to negotiate. The subsequent "fee" was lowered to $62. Customs then customs tacked on a daily storage fee of $30.

~ Anonymous

United Relocations[29]

United Relocations is a Singaporean based company recommended to me by many expats. Not only do they offer door to door service, the movers will even unpack and arrange your furniture removing the packaging materials on their way out. Talk about a hassle-free move. They also have a good working relationship with Customs which can save you time, stress, and money. Various international shipping companies utilize United Relocations for the Thai side of importations. sales.th@united-relo.com

Seven Seas Worldwide[30]

Seven Seas offers door to door shipping via, you guessed it, the sea. They also offer free packaging and storage for up to four weeks before you ship, so you can take a pre-relocation holiday. Seven Seas automatically provides basic insurance up to $160.00 for each box or suitcase lost. However, this does not cover partial loss of contents.

---

[29] http://bit.ly/unitedrelo

[30] http://bit.ly/7seasship

Their website has an instant quote generator which I tested. USA – Thailand (85 days transit) door to door for two large boxes was $365.88. Their quote includes Customs clearance. Their proposal has a warning that door to port doesn't include Customs fees, consider yourself warned.

Don't let all the stories scare you from moving your stuff to your new home. If you find a good company and aren't trying to cheat Customs, then things will go smoothly and in 10-12 weeks your cherished belongings will becoming part of your new life in Thailand.

TIP

Shipping through the post doesn't bypass Customs. A friend asked his mom to ship him a camera purchased on Amazon. She accidentally included the receipt in the package, and he was fined the cost of the camera (around $300) for bringing it in.

United States Postal Service

For smaller packages or lighter items, you can use the postal service. Thailand's postal system is efficient, easy to use, and you can track your package until it's in your hands. You can ship items to a hotel, guest house, or local post office. I was quoted $174 USD for a 15kg (33 lb) box for domestic arrival 5 days later.

The postal system imposes a different set of importation rules than the ports. You are required to declare how much the package is worth and its contents. Items are rarely opened if valued under $33, however, if they suspect illegal importation, they will inspect the package. If they find you guilty of tax evasion, shipping in that new camera as a 'used book,' you will be fined heavily. Once again, honesty really is the best policy.

Upon collection, expats have reported that occasionally postal staff request a few notes for all their hard work. Once I picked up a Christmas gift sent from my mother, the manager called me aside and mumbled something about $12. Knowing where he was going, I very politely said thank you, picked up the packet, and walked out.

TIP
If it's valuable, take it on the plane. Furthermore, put it in your carry on, the TSA is no better than Customs.

SHIP LATER

Some expats arrive in Thailand without any idea where they will live. They have nothing more than a vague plan. Others know the city they are relocating to but not much more. The latter can ship to a town's main post office. The former can cash in some favors with family and friends through the storage of a few boxes or rent a storage space for a few months until they make more concrete plans.

I highly recommend visiting a variety of cities, trying them on for size, for at least a month or two before you select where to move. Keep in mind that the more you lug with you, the harder it will be each time you move.

BY PLANE, YOUR PLANE

Almost all younger expats opt to whittle down their belongings to what they can carry and check on their flight, knowing that whatever they need upon arrival, they can purchase in Thailand. Some expats become minimalists after cleaning out their belongings for the move, they enjoy the freedom and opt to only use what is necessary to maintain their life.

Moving with kids is understandably harder, but still doable. Check with your airline for the price of a second or third suitcase (usually around $100-200) and decide what route makes the most sense for you and yours.

WHAT TO LEAVE AT HOME

You can drastically thin out your winter clothes collection. You won't need it for Thailand, however, if you plan to continue a quest of world exploration, keep a few key pieces of winter gear. After you adapt to the warm weather, you may need a light jacket during trips to the mountains, inside shopping malls, and in cinemas (where the AC is cranked way up).

If you usually travel with a medical kit or a pharmacy in your purse, know that you shouldn't have to stock up on common over the counter products. You can buy diarrhea tablets, aspirin, paracetamol, birth control, plasters, mosquito repellent, and most other medical requirements at the counter in 24 hour pharmacies.

I really recommend you leave the hair straighteners and curlers at home. It's way too hot to style your hair with hot appliances, and the humidity will destroy all of your work in a matter of minutes. Don't fight the tropics, it always wins.

SHIPPING YOUR WHEELS

Just like shipping your stuff, shipping your vehicle isn't easy or cheap but it's possible. There are two routes to bringing a car or motorbike – temporary or permanent. If you want to drive the length of Thailand in a sports car or on a BMW bike, consider a temporary import or renting your wheels. If you are attached to your car and consider it part of the family, or believe strongly that you cannot find the same quality vehicle in Thailand then consider importing it. If you're looking for an everyday vehicle to get from point A to B than buy a car in Thailand.

TEMPORARY

Bringing a car or bike into Thailand temporarily (up to 6 months) is straight forward and can be accomplished with a tourist visa. You'll need an international driver's license and the title and insurance for the vehicle. In addition, you will need a re-export contract that will require a deposit which you can recoup after the vehicle is re-exported.

PERMANENT

Shipping permanently is more complex.

You:
- must have owned the vehicle for at least 18 months
- must have a non-immigrant visa (and usually a work permit)
- can't rent the car out or sell it for the first 3 years
- need an import permit from the Ministry of Commerce
- need an import permit for second hand cars from the Foreign Trade Department of the Ministry of Commerce before the vehicle arrives

In addition to the paperwork, you will pay duties and tax on the vehicle. Customs calculates the fee's with a CIF value (Cost & Insurance & Freight). There is no way to tell the exact cost of the CIF until you get to the port. Sometimes Customs calculates based on the current value of the car, sometimes on the original price of the car. They have their own rule sheet that is designed to benefit them.

A used car averages $3,000 - $6,000. Import taxes can potentially match that cost. Because of this, very few expats opt to ship their car. In addition to expense and logistical stress, the mechanics aren't as experienced with international car care and maintenance, nor will they carry your parts.

Shipping Companies

Motorbikes (recommended by GT rider)
http://www.fairandeasy.co.th/motorcycles.html

Cars:
http://www.bangkokshipping.com/shippingcars.php
http://www.pattayashipping.com/carship.php

GT rider is an excellent resource for additional information pertaining to motorcycle rentals and importation.

SELLING YOUR CAR

A few weeks before your move start advertising. Carmax is always an excellent last minute option since they'll give you an offer within an hour. They'll also set up the paperwork with a buy offer that's good for a week. So you can get the figure, then return a week later when you're ready to ship off.

Selling your car also gives you some instant cash to spend exploring your new home.

GADGETS & TECHNOLOGY

STREAMING MUSIC AND MOVIES

With the cost of living so low, you might find you have more free time to enjoy movies or listen to music. While Netflix doesn't have the copyright privileges to operate in Thailand, it's possible to run a program that makes it seem like you're in the United States. A VPN, or IP bouncer program, does just that. Some programs cost a few dollars and others are free. I've used a free program called <u>Hotspot Shield</u>[31] without problems. I just opened Hotspot Shield and typed in <u>netflix.com</u> or <u>pandora.com</u>, and I can stream movies and tunes from Thailand.

Spotify works in Thailand but only if you buy the premium package ($10 a month). The cheaper packages will allow you to have 'vacation time' but ends your vacation after two weeks. Using the VPN program will also solve this problem.

---

[31] <u>http://bit.ly/VPNblck</u>

BEST APPS FOR EXPATS

Technology really has changed expat life. Gone are the days of expensive international pay-phone calls, international calling cards, and the inability to keep in touch with loved ones. You don't even need to buy maps, or carry pocket dictionaries anymore! The following list is the most helpful apps for expats in Thailand:

Facebook – Even if FB wasn't part of your life before you became an expat, you will see how helpful it is to keep in touch with loved ones at home. You can find many needed resources and referrals from more experienced expats in your area through FB groups. There are also many buy and sell trading groups that function just like Craigslist. I bought my motorbike off one and have sold many items in these groups.

Skype – Free calls to other Skype accounts anywhere in the world, very economic calls to any cell or landline, and free video calls. It's the best way to keep in touch with loved ones at home. In addition to the free features, you can purchase a personal number so others can keep in contact with you without paying international fees

Line – Is a widely used social app in Thailand. It's useful for free internet messages and group chats. You're sure to hear Thais and expats ask you "what's your line?"

What's App – an even more popular instant messaging service. If your new friend has a smart phone and doesn't have line they'll most likely have What's App.

Google Maps – is especially useful when you arrive. Thailand's streets and soi's (*avenues*) can be confusing and most Thai's can't give directions to save their lives, even if you present a map.

Maps with Me - is an offline version of Google maps and great if you don't have internet access.

Speedtest – While internet is everywhere, rarely is it fast or reliable. Digital nomads like to run speed tests everywhere they go.

XE currency - perfect for when your brain just isn't calculating correctly. A useful app that also comes in handy when haggling as you can show the seller a figure and go from there.

Kindle – There are plenty of used bookstores in Thailand, however, if you're picky about what you read or don't want to lug all your books around, then a Kindle is a must. You can download books with a click and carry hundreds of titles with you when you travel. Plus, they just released Kindle Unlimited, a $9.99 monthly subscription program that allows unlimited downloads and reading.

Trip Advisor – Find restaurants, hotels, and the best attractions a city has to offer with this app. Thailand is represented very accurately by expats and tourists alike.

Dropbox – A great way of safely storing information, documents, and photos. Simply download the app and then drop items into the box. Everything is stored virtually (and safely) allowing you to access your dropbox from any computer in the world. You can also share folders (bigger than what you can share via email). You're given 2GB of free storage but can expand it by referring other people or by purchasing 1TB for $9.99 a month.

Thai keyboard – Make sure you download a Thai keyboard on your smartphone so you can type Thai words. Essential for the next two apps.

Google Translate – lets you translate words or sentences from English into Thai. It will also translate web pages if you're using Google Chrome. The translations between Thai and English are not exact but they usually will get the job done.

Weather Bug - While the weather in Thailand is easy to gauge by looking out the window, you will be best served to keep this app in your phone for when you plan long motorbike routes or want to keep up with loved ones at home dealing with snow and ice storms.

Thai Dictionary – It's useful to find Thai words or find a translation. Make sure you also download a keyboard

Angry birds – The game is incredibly popular in Thailand! If you've never played it, prepare to get hooked.

Moving Checklist

✦ Put your house on the market for sale/rent
✦ Secure your visa at the Thai Embassy
✦ Make sure furry family members' paperwork is in order
✦ Decide what is staying and what is going
✦ Get quotes from moving companies (at least two companies and follow up on their references)
✦ Secure contact information for each stage of the shipment process
✦ Open a frequent flyer account and book your flight

Moving Day

✦ Double check the inventory and the condition, make sure items are marked as used
✦ Confirm your Thai shipping address
✦ Keep the receipt in a safe place
✦ Update your contact details with the movers as soon as you get to Thailand

AFTER YOU ARRIVE

As so perfectly put in the <u>Costa Rica</u> edition of the *Becoming an Expat* guidebook series:

"Welcome to your new life as an expat. Make sure to take in this moment, celebrate it! Don't rush past it, you are no longer in a hurry. Settle into the rhythm of the country."

WHERE TO LAND

If this is your first time in Thailand, you're going to encounter many new things. The language and cultural barriers in addition to the tropical climate is a lot to adjust to all at once. Be patient with yourself. Fortunately, since Thailand is setup for tourism, there are plenty of resources to help you adjust.

I recommend staying in Bangkok for a few days to stave off your jet-lag. After reading the **What Region is Best for You** section of this book, you should have an idea where you want to live or a few cities you'd like to check out.

It's a good idea to find a temporary base. Rent a flat or guest house for a month and explore from there. You can leave the bulk of your belongings and travel lightly around neighboring islands or provinces. This is the best way to determine which city is best suited for you.

If you're coming to Thailand for work, head to the city where you've received employment a week or two before you start work to secure housing and settle in.

FINDING HOUSING

Condominiums are easy to find so make sure you look at a handful of places before you put down a deposit. Take a day, drive or walk around the area you want to be in, and when you see a nice apartment block, go in and ask about available rooms. Even if you don't see a 'for rent' sign ask, many places don't advertise. Also, utilize the expat community. Ask which areas or buildings are most desirable and why. You can expect to pay a deposit in order to secure the room, often $94 - $157. When moving in, you'll pay the first month's rent plus one or two month's security deposit (refunded at the end).

Finding a house to rent is a bit more tricky. I would still recommend driving around the various neighborhoods so you can decide which areas appeal to you the most. Then you'll have a starting point when you approach a real estate agent. He or she should be able to find some good options within your budget. Sometimes the house hunt takes a few days, especially if you have special requirements. When you find a place that suites your needs, don't dabble, secure it. The smaller cities have less inventory, therefore are a bit more challenging to find your perfect match.

TIP
The Thai word for rent is *chao*.

GATHERING YOUR BEARINGS

Explore Thailand like a tourist. Take pictures, try the local foods, and embrace the moment (and the smells that come with it). The novelty will eventually wear off and you will settle into your new stride. Do your best to remain open and flexible as you find your pace in your new Thai life. Many expats get caught up comparing how things here are different to their home country. It can really hinder your overall experience.

Get connected in the expat community. Not only will you understand Thailand better but you'll also see how comfortably and happily well adapted expats are living. You might also see some examples of how not to be.

GETTING CONNECTED

COMMUNICATION

SIM CARDS

7 - 11 sells prepaid sim cards that don't expire and pay for themselves since the $9.40 fee to purchase them is credited to your account. The most reliable providers are True Move, AIS, and 12-Call.

UNLOCKED AND LOADED

American phones are almost always locked to a provider and sim. In order to use a different (Thai) sim in your phone, it first must be unlocked. There is a new law that requires cell phone providers to unlock your phone if you have a zero balance, are not under contract, and have paid off your phone. Contact your provider to find out how to go about unlocking the phone.

If you're unsuccessful unlocking your phone in your home country, it's easy to find a shop in Thailand that can help you (even with iPhones). Bangkok has shops all over the tourist circuit that unlock phones for under $10. Or, if you just want to pick up a basic Nokia phone (brick), they start at just $10. Make sure you cancel your contract with your service provider before you leave the country.

3G & DATA

True Move currently offers the best coverage and runs about $12.50 for 1GB. If you want to be connected everwhere, then this is one of your best options. Sometimes foreigners encounter trouble with their data plan on their tablets or smart phones. If this happens to you, check your APN settings (google where this can be found on your device). It should automatically adjust but in case it doesn't, below is a list of APN settings for each provider:

True Move
Name: TrueMove H Internet
APN: internet
Username: true
Password: true

AIS/ One-2 call
APN settings
username: (blank)
password: (blank)
APN name: internet

DTAC (GPRS)
APN settings
username: (blank)
password: (blank)
APN name: www.dtac.co.th

INTERNET

It won't be hard to find internet in Thailand. It's one of the most connected countries in the world and has the heaviest Facebook use. Free wifi is available in most cafes and restaurants. Cloud internet is available for just $3.13 a month for unlimited access to basic internet at any hotspot across the city.

Many apartments and hotels offer internet (free or for a monthly fee). If you rent a house, you will need to install it yourself and sign a year contract. Basic monthly internet costs you between $9.40 - $19.00, and fiber optic cable will set you back $38.00 a month. I highly recommend the fiber optic if you work from home.

PROVIDERS

3BB and True Move offer internet packages (check what's best where you live). They each offer free installation but you may need a Thai friend to help translate (the technicians speak limited English).

OTHER

Skype, Line and Whats App all offer free messaging and calls to other accounts (see the *Best Apps for Expats* section for more info).

NOW THAT YOU'RE CONNECTED, GET CONNECTED

Finding friends and engaging with the expat community is essential to your enjoyment of Thailand. Eating at street stalls, going on motorbike trips, and getting lost in Bangkok is all more fun with friends. If you moved with your life partner, then you have a head-start over the rest of the expats. The expat community in Thailand is welcoming and helpful to newbies.

When I arrived in Chiang Mai, I barely knew a soul. It only took a few dinners and cocktails before new friendships began to blossom. Oftentimes you are adopted into a group of friends. One friend can become ten overnight. A yoga class, sports team practice, or expat meet-up could be the first day of you and a new best friend's life together.

TIP
A simply smile and greeting is the key to thriving in Thailand.

LEARN THE LINGO

Thai is not the easiest language to learn but if you try, you'll be rewarded. Thais love it when foreigners can say a few words or crack a joke. But where to begin? Well *Sawadee* (hello) is a good place to start, followed by *Kup koon ka/kup* (thank you). The best thing to learn right off the bat are numbers and your favorite food dishes for when the restaurant doesn't have an English menu. Since Thailand is tourist friendly, many expats never learn Thai. I highly recommend you do your best and learn as much as you can because you will to integrate more successfully. See the last section in this book for the most useful Thai words to get you started.

How do you learn best?

If you're like me, a visual learner, pick up <u>Thai for Beginners</u> by Benjawan Poom Becker. It's a good place to start. It teaches you the most common words and sentences in 10 easy lessons. If you're an auditory learner then soak in as much Thai spoken around you as possible.

If you need extra motivation or want more guidance with enunciation and tones (many a time I've used the wrong tone and said penis to a man selling bananas. It's the same word in Thai) then take a class. Thai teachers often speak perfect English and can explain Thai grammar in ways easy to remember. Thai classes are also a great place to make new friends.

Finally, the tried and tested best way to learn Thai is to date one. Of course this method only works for single expats, but it's a great motivator when you can't figure out what your girlfriend / boyfriend is saying behind your back to their family.

GETTING AROUND

RENT OR BUY A MOTORCYCLE

You can save a lot of money in the long run by investing in a means of transportation. Plus you'll see more of the country and discover areas that aren't heavily trafficed by public transit.

After you've found your feet in Thailand and explore your immediate area, decide which means of transportation will work best for you. Don't rush the decision. If you're considering buying a moto, rent one first. Plan your route from the shop, avoid busy and traffic congested areas, and plan to go somewhere where you can drive with ease. Don't forget your helmet!

Once you feel comfortable on the bike, rent it for the week or the month (monthly is cheaper). If you don't like that particular bike, try a different brand. Honda Clicks make great beginner bikes. Confirm the brakes are sufficient before you leave the shop. After a week or month riding on your moto, you will have a good idea if it's the mode of transport for you.

Motos are super economical and are easy to resell if you have a change of heart or decide to explore another country down the road. With $470 - $780 you can pick up a decent used motorbike. You'll find a healthy moto market within the expat community.

If you want more engine power than the average moto, like a Honda CBR250 or full size motorcycle, I urge you to consider how often you will need the larger engine, and calculate the cost vs. the rental price (around $31 a day). Big bikes aren't as city friendly as moto bikes. Make sure you can park it securely with a wheel lock or other device. If you're a serious rider have a blast, if not, I recommend motos.

TIP

"When you get here - get a motorbike. It is the number one thing that will increase your quality of life here. You can get anywhere within minutes and zoom past traffic. If you're going to be in one place for more than 3 months - buy a used one. You will have your money back in 3-5 months, compared to wasting money on renting every month. Plus when you sell it, you usually get all of your money back. It's hard to go wrong."

~ Johan Pellsater, Swedish, Digital Nomad

BUY A CAR

More than likely, I talked you out of shipping your car in the *Before You Arrive* section. So how does one go about buying a car in Thailand? If you're looking for a used car, I recommend starting your hunt by perusing Facebook, Craigslist, classifieds (Bangkok Post, Phuket Gaette, Pattaya Mail), thaicar.com, ThaiSecondhand.com, or visiting a local car market. Keep in mind each car should come with the vehicle's Blue Book *(Lem Tabian)* that states who the present and past owners are, their addresses, and records of taxes paid on the vehicle.

You can buy a car with any visa, including a tourist visa, however, you will need a work permit or a *certificate of residence*. They are easy to obtain. Just present a housing rental contract, to an immigration office or embassy, and prove you have at least 30 days left on your passport. If you purchase it at immigration, you'll pay $15 USD, if you choose the embassy it will run you $80 USD.

Purchase a new car directly from the dealer. Most dealers will require full payment upfront. However, if you have a work permit and can prove steady income, you might be eligible for financing but you'll need to put a hefty 30-50% down payment. If you finance, you won't receive the Blue Book until the car is paid off. They will provide you a copy in the meantime.

REGISTRATION

Once you've found a car or motorbike that suits you, you need to fill out paperwork in order to transfer the blue ownership book to your name. All registration procedures and transfers of vehicle ownership are completed at the local Department of Land Transport Office (DLT).[32] Most new car dealerships will assist you

---

[32] http://bit.ly/Thaidmv

by issuing all of the necessary paperwork to the DLT. To find the nearest DLT see http://bit.ly/thaidmvlocations.

In order to transfer the vehicle in your name you'll need:

✦ The Blue Book (Green Book for Motorbikes)
✦ (If the seller or buyer is Thai) their I.D card and House Registration document (*Tabien Ban*)
✦ (If the seller or buyer is an expat) signed copies of their passport, visa, and work permit, or official confirmation of residency from either the Thai Immigration Bureau or their embassy
✦ Signed *Department of Land Transport Transfer* (of ownership) *Request* form
✦ If the car is over seven years old (or five for motorbikes), it must pass a roadworthiness test each year. If it has an up-to-date tax sticker (mentioned later in Registration), that proves it has done so
✦ Copies of each document

Make certain you have all of the transfer paperwork signed by the previous owner prior to providing payment. I highly recommend that you go to the DLT together in order to accomplish this. If you purchase new from a dealer, they'll handle most of the paperwork including the Blue Book, but you'll still need to provide a visa and certificate of residence.

When you sell the vehicle, make sure the new owner signs a contract stating they are the new owner of the vehicle. That way, if they crash it or cause harm, the police won't come after you.

INSURANCE

Liability insurance, or Compulsory Motor Insurance (CMI or *Por Ror Bor*), is required and can be purchased at: the DLT, a car dealership, or an insurance company. This insurance is paid annually and must remain active. It covers the medical cost of those you may injure, but it doesn't cover any vehicle damage.

For those who would like some protection for their own skin and / or property, there are higher levels of insurance available. They are designated by class: 1st class, 2nd class, and 3rd class. First class is the highest and considered fully comprehensive. Second class covers collision damage, and third class covers life and injury of those involved in the accident (including the occupants of your car).

To get an idea how much each level of insurance costs, I recommend you start with an insurance broker site like: bit.ly/Thaicarinsurance. Compare what is quoted with local insurance offices in your area. Always ask for client references and call them. Ask what their experience was like using the insurance.

TAX (Window Sticker)

Regardless of the type of vehicle, they all require a tax payment annually, similar to renewing tags in North America. Each year you will need to pay the tax prior to your window sticker expiration. Simply bring the Blue (or Green) Book and proof of CMI coverage to a local DLT office.

DRIVER'S LICENSE

Entering Thailand with a foreign license will remain satisfactory for up to a year if the license has a photo, is in English (or translated in English), and has been issued by a country that has a treaty with the Thai government (US, Canada, Australia, New Zealand, and the UK are covered). However, you will need to secure a Thai license if will have a non-immigrant visa. Don't worry, you won't be stuck taking a road test again if you have an internationally recognized license (as mentioned above).

TIP
The deadline to secure your Thai license is one year after your arrival, but if you have a comprehensive Thai insurance policy it may become void after three months of driving on a foreign license.

To pick up your Thai driver's license, you will need to go to your DLT with:

+ Passport with valid non-immigrant visa
+ Work permit, or a Certificate of Residence issued by the Thai Immigration Bureau, or a Letter of Residence issued by the appropriate embassy. The work permit must be valid and the letter or certificate no more than 30 days old
+ Medical certificate from a hospital or health clinic no more than 30 days old
+ Two photographs, 1x1 inch, no more than six months old. In some offices photos are not required because they take them in-shop with DLT cameras
+ Valid international or foreign driving license
+ Copies of all the above docs
+ Fee

If you come equipped before 8:30am, the entire process can be completed in 3-5 hours. That, of course, depends on how busy they are when you show up. Some offices are so busy, they turn people away at 9am. The required forms must be completed in Thai, so take along a Thai speaker for interpretation and assistance filling out the forms. That being said, there are offices that accommodate English speakers. The Chatuchak office employes English-speaking staff to assist you making the entire process English-friendly.

You will need to take an eyesight exam and reaction test, so bring your best glasses and drink your coffee. When the paperwork is complete, the fee is paid, and your exams are satisfactory, you will be issued a Thai driver's license valid for one year. Upon renewal, your second license could be valid for five years. It seems officials are not equal, some grant a five year license others only allow for one additional year.

If you have a *motorcycle* endorsement on your license, it will automatically grant you a motorcycle license in Thailand. Your motorcycle license does not have a restriction on the engine size.

PUBLIC TRANSIT

If renting or buying a motorbike or car doesn't appeal to you, read about Thailand's public transportation in the **Basics** section. If you're adventurous, you could try and take a different mode of public transportation everyday for a week. Below are a few of your options:

BTS Sky Train
Bangkok Metro
Thai Airways
State Railway of Thailand
BKS Bus Service
Royal Automobile Association of Thailand

RECEIVING YOUR STUFF

If you packed all of your belonging via an airplane, you're all set. If you hired a company to ship a few boxes or a container, it's a good idea to call your moving company a few days before the estimated arrival date to check their progress. Upon arrival to Customs, make sure you bring a translator to pay your import fees and taxes. Expect this process to take a few days.

If you live in a condo, alert the staff on moving day so they can help point movers in the right direction, otherwise keep a look out for the truck (especially if you live on a small avenue).

FURNISHING & DECORATING

If you're moving into rented accommodations, half of the time it's fully furnished. You can ask that the furniture be removed but it's cheaper and easier to work with what you get. The key to furnishing your place is to *set a budget* and *make a list of what you need*. Thailand sells numerous gorgeous decorations for your home.

For kitchenware and bedding, head to a Tesco Lotus or Big C. These supermarkets sell kettles, cutlery, plates etc. For more unique items, such as silk pillowcases and wooden sculptures, head to the local weekend handicraft market. Most cities have a weekend *walking street*. In Bangkok there's JJ Market – A giant weekend market full of amazing things to fill your home.

All over Thailand there are the cheap *brick'a'brack* shops that sell almost everything. Need plastic boxes, coat hangers, brooms, or plates? They have them. You'll know you have arrived when you see an open shop overflowing onto the sidewalk with plastic merchandise!

In larger communities, check out the Facebook groups and Craigslist. There are always people selling off their stuff cheap on their way out of the country.

ESTATE PLANNING

It's important to get your affairs in order before you leave home. Take the time to think about what will happen to your assets and your family if you die. Sure, it's morbid, but focus on the organization of your assets instead of your demise. It's much easier on your loved ones if you plan for the inevitable. Create a legal will in both your home country and Thailand, covering the assets in the corresponding country.

Look for a referral from the expat community for a good estate planning attorney in Thailand. If you're moving with a spouse make sure each of you knows the other's wishes, including your burial or cremation preference. Flying a body internationally is extremely expensive if you don't have repatriation insurance. Also, if there are situations where you don't want to be resuscitated (i.e. intubation, feeding tube, etc) meet with your doctor and create a Living Will. Then, make sure your loved ones know your wishes and where the Living Will is located.

If you've leased land in Thailand, the contract dies with you unless you appoint an heir. Siam Legal[33] offers free advice and assistance drafting Thai wills. Your Thai Last Testimony will cover your assets in Thailand including: property, bank accounts, vehicle(s), and personal items. It's tempting to have your personal attorney draft a Thai will for you in addition to your home country because you are comfortable with your estate planning attorney. However, an internationally created will covering Thai assets could be problematic and burdensome for your family who are the ones left to deal with the documentations that need to be translated, notarized, and approved by a government body. This is why I highly recommend you have a separate Thai will for your assets in Thailand.

---

[33] http://bit.ly/thaiwills

LOGISTICS CHECKLIST

✦ Sort your debts, set up direct debit to repay them
✦ Check your passport validity, prepare important documents (including copies)
✦ Gather immigration documents and apply for a visa
✦ Get the necessary shots for your pup & for you
✦ Set up a mail solution
✦ Tell your bank you will be accessing your money from abroad, or open a new account that is better suited for your international life
✦ Sort your stuff into what to take, what stays in storage and what to sell, then try to halve your piles the second time around
✦ Sell your high dollar stuff on eBay, have a yard sale, or give things to charity
✦ If shipping a container, get quotes from at least 3 movers for door to door shipping
✦ Arrange for a pick up
✦ If shipping your car, arrange the paperwork, get at least 3 quotes from shipping companies and ask for references
✦ If selling your car, start advertising and see what your local used car dealers will give you. Check with Carmax if there is one near you
✦ Buy any essentials you think you need in Thailand (e.g. underwear, shoes, specific vitamins, cosmetics, etc.)
✦ Book your flight

SINGLES & DATING

This chapter is a helpful guide to understand the Thai dating scene. It can help you stay single if that's what you want, or find your match. If you're already happily hitched, feel free to skip forward to the *Family & Education* section, or read about what your single expat buddies endure for love.

DATING

Despite the abundance of good looking folks parading around Thailand in short skirts and with perfectly styled hair, dating in Thailand is a whole new ball game.

There are hundreds of *farang* men with Thai ladies. You'll see two main categories; overweight men in their 60s grasping hold of 20 year olds in miniskirts who are ignoring them, and couples who clearly love and support one another.

LOOKING FOR MRS. RIGHT?

You have the pick of the litter. Not only can you date Thai women, but you'll also have access to an abundant expat community filled with beautiful foreign ladies. You will need to keep your senses alert. Some Thai women use farangs like ATMs. You've heard of an Mrs. degree? Well they have a profession based around reeling in North Americans. Not all girls are like this, but there is a certain type so use your common sense if she seems really into you. If you go on a Thai date, her friends will come with her and you'll be expected to pay for them all. I have heard the complaint of shallow relationships and that it was hard to have a conversation with a deeper meaning than your next meal. Again, not all Thai girls lack depth but I find the most successful Thai-Expat relationships are when the Thai has lived abroad as well.

Thai's judge on fun rather than age. I've met many people in successful relationships with a 10-15 year age difference. Plus, being chubby is a positive feature in Thailand, it shows you enjoy eating which is very important in Thai culture.

EXPAT EXPERIENCE

"I came for the climate, the affordability, the digital nomad/expat community, and the hot girls (no, not the prostitutes, I'm not old and creepy). I'm staying for all the same reasons plus many more.

The dating scene leaves more to be desired, unless you're in the cities. In the places where I've lived (Krabi and Chiang Mai), I've noticed there are four groups of people. In the order from fewest to the most, there are expats, tourists, Thai people who speak English and Thai people who don't speak English.

There aren't enough eligible expats around, unless you're in Bangkok. That leaves English speaking Thai people, however, if you learn Thai you're guaranteed to increase your chances of meeting and dating awesome people. Also, get yourself set up with LINE (the app) once you get here. Thais and expats alike run their social lives through this app."

~ Johan Pellsater, Digital Nomad

LOOKING FOR MR. RIGHT?

I have good news and bad news for you. The dating scene in Thailand is saturated with foreign men chasing Thai girls and Thai men too shy to talk to you or not willing to cross the cultural barriers. However, it's a rich environment for self development and reliance. I have met numerous strong, inspirational expat folks here. Once you stop worrying about finding a partner, he will likely enter your life. In the meantime, you can focus on yourself and what you enjoy doing. Try yoga, thai chi, or another new hobby.

EXPAT EXPERIENCE

"I moved here with my boyfriend and at first, I was slightly uncomfortable when we went to a bar. There would be scantily clad women gyrating on poles in front of your drinks. I don't feel threatened by these girls, I feel sorry for them. There is a different mentality in Thailand regarding sex workers. It's a common sight here. We eventually found a few places that are strictly non "girly bars" so we no longer are harassed with the same broken questions or asked to buy the girls drinks."

~ Melanie Long, Mermaid Performer & Underwater Model/Stunt actress

---

LGBT EXPATS

There's a healthy LGBT community all over Thailand. Thais are open when it comes to gender, preferences, and partner choice. They leave the sexual stereotyping at the border. Chiang Mai is nicknamed the San Francisco of Thailand. The dating scene is more lively for men than women, sorry girls!

COUPLES

Arriving in Thailand as a couple is ideal of course. You have someone to experience this exotic country with. Thais love to see couples and will usually give you an even bigger grin.

TIP
Shows of public affection, touching, and kissing in public is somewhat taboo here. As a foreigner, you can do it but be aware that Thais don't even hold hands in public. They have a subtler way of touching. Be mindful of this, and while they offer you some forgiveness, respect their culture.

FAMILY

Bringing your family to Thailand is a big decision. Uprooting them and moving to the other side of the world seems daunting but this section will show you how it's done with the guidance of others who have made the move and paved the way for you. We understand that where you choose to raise your kids and live as a family is a personal decision, so we are simply here to show you the pros and cons, not sell you towards or away from the idea.

Some of the pros of raising your children abroad are teaching them how to adapt to a new way of life and meeting kids from another culture thus deepening their understanding of the world and what encompasses it. They'll learn they're not rooted to one town, and later in life if they don't like their situation, they're not stuck, they have the ability to change it. I grew up abroad as a child and I'm very grateful for the experiences it afforded me (although I do remember shedding a few tears on the first day of my new school).

I have great childhood memories, including remembering my parents were relaxed and lived in a higher standard of living than when we were in the UK. My childhood memories abroad just seem brighter.

With the current discontent of life in the USA, UK, and with Canada's cold weather, why not consider a richer more affordable life for your family by moving abroad? Debt won't solve itself overnight, however, I've met many families who made it work by renting out their home, moving to Thailand, and now live a much easier life.

The cons include: language barrier, slow social integration for your kids, culture shock, feeling as if they are outsiders, andunknowns regarding the quality of education and how it will effect your child's opportunities later in life. Every child reacts differently to a new environment, only you know your children best. Some kids thrive with this challenge and new way to live, others can become reclusive and resentful.

EXPAT EXPERIENCE

"I liked the idea of raising an open-minded child, which I think is the result of a child that experiences different cultures. There are children from 35 different countries at my daughter's school, so she's exposed not only to Thai culture, but many others too. It makes a tolerant person and one not bound by preconceived ideas. It's also very safe here. Being on an island means we have the benefits of a small town community without the narrow-mindedness of small town mentality. There's also a large expat community and people that are open to travel are generally broad-minded."

~ Rosanne Turner, regular contributor for Samui Holiday Magazine and co-owner of TEFL training centre www.samuitefl.com

---

Daliah offered to tell me about why she decided to raise her children in Thailand:

EXPAT EXPERIENCE

"I love life here, I love what I do, and my kids get to play outside everyday. Most neighborhoods have houses with their own pools or shared pools. The children feel safe and aren't exposed to many of the things in the west. I don't worry about too much consumerism, TV, advertisements, etc. I'm not stressed so the kids also feel calm and secure.

They love the beach, nature, animals that visit our garden, the sounds of the island, the fact that everything is accessible to them, and they get to partake in endless activities."

~ Dahliah, runs holistic centres on Koh Samui and Koh Phangan
www.Orionretreat.com

ACCLIMATING THE KIDS

Settling the children into their new expat life may very well be the hardest part of moving to Thailand. However, since Thailand is a family friendly country, settling in shouldn't be too difficult.

Before you leave home, show your kids some of the fun activities they can do in Thailand. It's important to get the kids onboard, because everyone will have to work to successfully acclimate. Call the parents of their best friends to discuss setting up Skype or email chat so your kids can keep in touch.

If this is your family's first time to Thailand, spend some time being a tourist. Spend a few days exploring your new home. Meet some locals (Thai's and elephants) so your children can see what their new home is all about.

TIP

Thais love children, especially blonde kids because it's an anomaly there as all Thais have black hair.

Let the kids be part of the moving process. Let them decide what toys to take and pack their own suitcase (you can always repack it secretly later). Ask them for their opinion while house hunting. Have them help you unpack the house. This will make them feel empowered and part of the process, not a floundering kid without a voice.

Make sure and plan a bunch of activities for the first month, so they adjust to the options available to them in their new home. Thailand has a wealth of family activities, from nature to adventure. Below are a few ideas to get you running:

✦ **Meet an elephant** – This is a must do for children. There are even sanctuaries that cater to children.

✦ **Visit a temple** – There are as many temples here as there are Starbucks in the States. Explore a few with your kids providing them a glimpse into the culture they are now living in. If possible, hire a guide and let your kids ask all the questions they want.

✦ **Go to the market** – The market is a great place to explore all of the new produce and Thai food.

✦ **Have a picnic by a waterfall** – Most cities in Thailand have nearby waterfalls with picnic grounds, bon appetite.

✦ **Visit the beach** – Getting to the beach is usually very affordable. Koh Chaang, Krabi and Koh Samui are all very family friendly.

✦ **Head to a hotel pool**- In northern Thailand, many of the hotels offer use of the pool for $3 per person.

✦ **Explore your neighborhood** – Take a walk and create a tick list of what to show your kids (e.g. 7-Eleven convenience store, water refilling machine, silver car, bird, stray dog, a flower).

✦ **Start (or continue) a family routine**- Do you always have Sunday lunch together? Watch a movie once a week? Do a weekly shop together? Just because you're in a new country doesn't mean family traditions have to change. If you don't have any weekly activities then why not start one?

TIP
Don't let your kids pet stray dogs. While they aren't aggressive, they're not accustomed to being touched and will react with a bark or a bite to anyone who comes near them.

EXPAT EXPERIENCE

"As I stood at Heathrow airport waiting for our flight to Bangkok, I thought, "What have we done?" My two young children were fighting around my legs while my wife argued with the check-in woman about seat allocation. The day before I had given away my Series 5 BMW to my brother and stored a full-size fibre glass statue of Bruce Lee in my sister's garage. Our comfortable life was about to change for good.

I suppose quality of life here depends what you are used to, how adaptable you are, and your expectations. Things won't be like home, you'll see a lot more rats at night around rubbish bins, it's fantastically hot, but everything is a lot cheaper, a lot busier and more chaotic. It's like someone turned up the brightness and volume on the TV.

When we first arrived we took our kids to the zoo a lot, not because they particularly liked it, but because it's fantastically cheap if you flash your work permit and have a stab at speaking Thai to the nice lady behind the booth. It's $0.62 for kids and $1.55 for adults... You show me a father in the world that wouldn't want to take advantage of that.

We also went to the Night Safari both during the day and at night. Our kids preferred it during the day because it was quieter and felt like you shouldn't really be there. We took them swimming in a variety of pools. If your kids like swimming pools, there are some great ones here in private gated villages.

There's also great restaurants that are children friendly, the one our kids like the most is the awkwardly named Khao Mao Kao Fang. Our children refer to it rather accurately as The Jungle Restaurant (it was designed by a botanist); good food, big space, waterfalls, fast service, and great fun. Order the 'Birthday Ice Cream' and your kids will love you forever.

Apart from that, here in Chaing Mai, there are adventure parks, theme restaurants with big ball pools, zip-lines, an ice skating rink, cinemas, sport academies of every persuasion, Swenson Ice Cream parlors, and the usual range of modern day distractions for young children and tired parents. Have fun!"

~ Alex Gunn, Counsellor, Life Change People

EDUCATION

On the surface Thailand's education system is booming. Upon closer inspection, however, there's a lot of criticism about the style and quality of teaching. There's little incentive to teach. Teachers are underpaid and under- appreciated. Almost any English speaker can become a teacher, regardless of qualifications.

The best teachers are snatched up by the international schools who offer an appealing benefits package. The style of teaching (repeat after me and memorize) stems from the difficult Thai writing system. With 5 ways to write any one word, the only way to learn is root memory. While foreigners are quick to criticize, the Thai Government is trying to improve the system, offering free education to all (targeting the hill tribes and immigrants), and have increased school budgets in order to hire foreign teachers. Thai kids graduate school with (arguably) more manners, grace, and tend to be less "high maintenance" than other international school kids.

TYPES OF SCHOOLS

◆ International
◆ Bilingual
◆ Private Thai
◆ Missionary
◆ Thai government

As an expat, your children cannot attend Thai schools. Unless one parent is Thai, a foreign child cannot attend a Thai school. This leaves a huge market for the international and bilingual schools who see the need and fill it by catering to expat children of all nationalities. There is a large range regarding price and quality, the most expensive schools aren't always the best ones.

All large cities in Thailand have at least one international school. Bangkok has around 60 international schools, Chiang Mai has 7, Phuket has 5 and there are even 2 on Samui Island! Rather than hunting for schools blindly, the International Schools Association of Thailand[34] has compiled a list of all international schools in Thailand, along with their curriculum, accreditation, address, website and phone number.

TIP
Some of the better schools have waiting lists, so if possible, start contacting schools before you arrive. Otherwise, you might not get your first choice.

HOW TO CHOOSE A SCHOOL?

Ensuring your child feels comfortable at school is a high priority. Make sure your child is included in the decision-making

---

[34] http://bit.ly/SchoolsThai

process. If he/she dislikes the school's atmosphere, he/she could hate going to school there.

It's important to check accreditation, subject options, exam results, and future opportunities (what students go on to do). The curriculum is also important. If you think your child will go to a US college then there's no point following a British curriculum. It will be harder to pass the college acceptance exams.

There is a variety of curriculums to choose from: British, American, IB, German, French, Japanese, Chinese, etc. If you're only planning on spending a few years in Thailand, make sure the curriculum matches up with your home country. This way, the kids can gain the experience of living overseas without disrupting their schooling.

FINDING A SCHOOL 101

+ Check the ISAT website for schools near you
+ Check the curriculum the schools in your area offer
+ Visit prospective school's websites for information (tuition, school year start times, previous education)
+ Contact schools to inquire about vacancies (make an appointment to visit if you are already in Thailand)
+ Discuss and make a family decision
+ Join the waiting list
+ Pay tuition (usually in advance to secure visa paperwork)
+ Buy new notebooks and pens in preparation for the new school year

TIP
Most international schools offer free education for 1-2 of your children if you teach for their school. Combining work and your child's education could save you a bundle.

EXPAT PARENT TESTIMONIALS

"The Thai school syllabus has room for improvement. I wanted my daughter to be exposed to Thai culture, which she is at the international school, but have an education that will open doors for her in the future. Just because we moved here, doesn't mean it's where she will choose to spend her adult life. I didn't want her education to limit where she chose to go to university. By being able to take her British SATs at the international school, she can attend any university, which wouldn't be the case had she attended a Thai school. I found her school by researching on the internet and then speaking to several parents at the school before deciding it was right for us."

~ Rosanne, www.samuitefl.com

"The education system is great! My son attends an international school, classes are small and the teachers are from the UK. Leon has a best friend and goes to many after school activities such as: tea kwan do, art class, and football training. He's happy and has a nice balance between academia and nature-based play."

~ Daliah, www.Orionretreat.com

"There's a huge gap between the international and the Thai educational system and values. Generally, we consider their teaching style to be outdated. Teachers usually write the lesson on the board, and then require students to copy it in their notebooks. Little emphasis is placed on problem solving or reasoning, but the focus is on memorizing. Also, learning English in a Thai school will result in mediocre results. I think that most foreigners would want their child learning in an international school because they offer up-to-date teaching practices and the possibility to reintegrate into a school in another western country along the way if needed. Some wealthy Thai parents choose to send their children to an International school for those reasons as well. For Thai students, daily Thai lessons are provided in order to follow the country's curriculum and cultivate their identity."

~ Julie Cousineau, Primary school teacher

"Prices depend upon the age and year group of your child, the older the student the more expensive it is. To give you a rough idea, at the time of writing, yearly fees for a student in Grade 6 or 7 range from $5,784 -$15,632 depending upon the school. The bilingual schools are much cheaper as they are essentially Thai schools with some lessons taught in English. Also, unlike the international schools, they follow the Thai academic calendar which is completely different from the "western" academic calendar.

No matter how old your child, make sure the school is accredited. Most schools in Thailand use the Western Association of Schools and Colleges as an inspectorate. It's an American international school accreditation board which does ensure a level of capability."

~ Alex Gunn, Author of A Year in Chiang Mai

"The education system in Thailand lacks innovation and values rote-learning and memorization as opposed to critical thinking. This is why Thai parents that can afford to, send their children to learn overseas. I am finishing up my dissertation at the moment. I did study for three months at Thammasat University but, with the exception of one class, I was not impressed by the teaching nor coursework."

~ Aaron Johnson, PHD candidate

ALTERNATIVE KINDERGARTENS & PRIMARY

While the international schools dominate the market for competitive primary and secondary eduction, there are some great alternative options for younger children. The following schools ensure that both Thai and international curriculum is covered so children can proceed on to either international or Thai schools after the completion of their primary.

Montessori

Montessori education is an alternative education idea and focuses on human and psychological development. Classrooms are mixed age and based around spontaneous movement and internal choices. Children learn by interacting with their environment and problem solving. There is a Montessori school in every major city. A simple Google web search of " Montessori + City" will bring up schools in your area.

Panyaden

Another praised primary school in the north, near Chiang Mai, is Panyaden. They focus on holistic teaching, *"We aim to cultivate a way of life, as well as an academic education. Buddhist culture and values are our basis for living together. We aim to nurture the physical, moral, emotional, and intellectual aspects of our children holistically and we see that for this to happen, home, school and community must cooperate together."* http://bit.ly/panyaden

HOME SCHOOLING

If you are based in a more rural part of Thailand or you plan on moving locations often, you might want to consider home schooling. There's a great article on whether or not you should home school here: bit.ly/homeschoolprocon.

Home schooling is becoming more popular worldwide and can take the social and performance pressures off your child. If you can afford not to work, then you gain the benefits from spending more time with your child. There's an increasing number of expats home schooling for various reasons: money, quality of education, child peers, and groups have been created in Bangkok to support other parents and arrange social gatherings. Below are a few examples:

✦ Yahoo group - Bangkokhomeschoolers
✦ Facebook -BangkokhomeschoolersPlus
✦ www.bambiweb.org/en

If your child is Thai or half-Thai, you'll need to register them as home-schooled. Thai Homeschool Association (www.thaihomeschool.org) is a great source for information.

HOW TO BEGIN

The most important aspect of home schooling is following a curriculum and ensuring your child can pass the final exams to gain admittance into their preferred university.

If you're new to home schooling, not to worry, there's numerous excellent resources at your disposal.

K-12.com

Offers online education programs that are fully accredited, tuition-based, and highly flexible, offering multiple start dates throughout the school year. All offer full-time enrollment for a diploma or enrollment in individual courses to provide families a variety of options. It's an interesting alternative to regular school and is not dependent on as much parent time.

HomeSchool.com

This online community has countless resources for you to connect with other homeschoolers and supplement your curriculum. It's a great place to start your homeschooling research.

VirtualEdu.org

Online classes starting at $69.96 USD a month for grades 6-12 for a fully accredited US based online school. Online classes include teacher support, lessons, homework, class discussions, and assessments. The difference is the activities occur over the internet at a time that is convenient for students.

Global Village School

An online school that offers accredited, customizable K-12 home schooling programs via online and text-based curriculum, complete with individualized teacher services. You have to pay per semester or year ($1,250 -1,750) but you're given lots of support and guidance.

If you're interested in learning what a Thai's take is on homeschooling, read a recent article published in the Bangkok Post: http://bit.ly/thaitake

TIP
If you enroll your children at a new school but have to wait until the new school term (due to the difference in academic calendars), home schooling can help you bridge the gap. The school will also be able to advise you on what subjects you're required to cover.

ADOPTION

Do you want to start a multi-cultural family? Adoption is possible in Thailand but it requires a lot of patience and paperwork. Justine Broadhurst - Bristow (South African and head teacher of a kindergarten in Phuket) tells us about her experience:

You mentioned you have an adopted son. I've heard that it's difficult for foreigners to adopt Thai children. Is that true? What paperwork is needed/hoops did you have to jump through?

"We were fortunate in that we came to adopt our son by first acting as his legal guardians from birth, and later applying to legally adopt him. This is not a conventional avenue towards adoption, and while it was really an emotional roller-coaster, not following the traditional 'through an agency' route, we were so fortunate to have our son from birth.

Adoption agencies advise you every step of the way and guide you through the process of international adoption; but waiting to be matched to a child can take many, many years. We adopted the other way around. We had a little child whom we loved and adored, and we had to feel our way blindly through a process in a foreign country and in a foreign language all by ourselves, without the benefit of advice or guidance. The procedures for adopting in Thailand meet international standards and requirements as they are party to The Hague Convention on International Adoptions.

Overall, I wouldn't say that it's difficult to adopt from Thailand but it's a long process."

EXPAT EXPERIENCE

"My favourite memory? Driving through insane monsoon rains, over 800km to Songkhla to meet our little newborn baby. We collected him from a flooding Hat Yai and decided to call him Noah. It was a priceless memory!"

~ Justine

HOW TO LIVE FOR FREE

Living in Thailand is almost like living for free. You can find simple cheap accommodations in all the cities and a good meal can cost as little as a buck.

Usually rent or housing is the largest expense, shortly followed by food. However, there are ways to get rid of those expenses. Living rent-free can be a great way to explore different regions of Thailand before committing to a city.

Whatever the reason you want to live for free, there are just two requirements – pack light and be open to whatever opportunities come your way.

HOUSE, HOTEL, & PET-SITTING

Pet-sitting is an amazing route to free rent. It requires little effort, and while it forces you to be less mobile, the payoff is worth it to many. Pet owners who wish to take a vacation but love their pets like their own kids need to make certain they'll be taken care of. They will offer free rent for those that will maintain the home and provide TLC and exercise regimens for the animals.

Owners will ensure all the food is in the house necessary to feed the animals, all you need to do is feed yourself and do all of the requested chores / animal activities requested by the owner.

The complexity and work required can vary greatly from job to job. One job may require that you give meds to a dog, cat, or horse 4 times daily. Other jobs might just request a warm body in the house for the dog to snuggle with.

House-sitting duties also vary from job to job. You might need to upkeep a huge vegetable garden, or massive estate. Another job just asks that you water the plants, gather the mail, and return the house as it was given to you. Many owners are wary to leave their houses sitting empty for long spans of time for fear of burglary (although burglaries are rare in Thailand). They're also worried to leave the house empty during the rainy season in case of flooding or the inevitable monsoon mold.

Homeowners look for house or pet sitters first through word of mouth. If that doesn't land them a trustworthy candidate, they turn to the internet:

TrustedHousesitters.com (prices quoted per month)

$19.99 3 month plan, $12.99 6 months, $7.49 for one year (That's $89.99 for potentially up to a year of free housing). Access to housesitting opportunities world wide.

Bangkok Post
Sign up for free to access to the classifieds, housesitting opportunities, and job listings.

Bangkok Craigslist
Craigslist has a variety of housesitting gigs, house-swaps, and short term rentals at discounted rates.

FACEBOOK GROUPS

Check city specific groups such as: "What's happening in Chiang Mai" and "Community Online Pin Board Koh Samui" or check real estate specific groups like "Bangkok, Take over my lease, short term rentals, and space sharing." Based on my research, this route is the number one way people find house or pet-sitters in Thailand.

MASTERING HOUSE/PET SITTING

First, you need to keep your ears open for opportunities. The busiest house/pet sitting seasons are December (Christmas holidays), April (Songkran holidays), and during the rainy season (escaping the rain and humid holidays).

The best house-sitting opportunities go fast, often within the first two days of being posted. Make sure you check the websites regularly, set up email alerts, and don't dilly-dally.

Landing the first house-sit is always the hardest so make sure your profile is optimal and demonstrates your personality and reliability. If you can't provide house-sitting references then offer job references, couchsurfing references, and character references instead.

It's key to demonstrate your responsibility, trustworthiness, and enthusiasm for the pet you would be watching (if applicable). Create a resume specific for each house/pet sit satisfying all of the owner's requests in the ad. If you have any special talents that could be applicable, mention them. For example, if you **have** a green thumb, mention it, if they run a B&B and you have marketing, design, or video production skills, mention it. If you're a handy man/woman, mention it.

Always be honest. Why do you want to stay in their home? Share with the owner your goals, ambitions, and how this house sit can play into them.

Finally don't forget to ask questions of your own. Clarify your responsibilities if you don't fully understand them. Ask if you can have guests over? How long can the pet be alone for? What's the internet situation? Where would you be permitted to sleep? Can you use the washing machine? What about the perishables in the fridge? Take a walk through the house with the owner before they go and make sure you know what you need to do. Also, make sure you have a contact number for them in case of emergencies. Offer to Skype with them every so often so they can see their home and / or pets.

TIP

In addition to having the house spic and span for their return, I like to have a casserole or brownie batch waiting for them. It's such a treat to arrive home to ready made food in the fridge after international travel. You're too tired to cook and usually just want to get home. Do this and you'll top their list of house-sitters and other offers will come pouring in.

COUCHSURFING

The easiest way to explore Thailand hotel-free is through CouchSurfing.org. It's a website and travel movement *hell-bent* to change the world *"one couch at a time"* as its slogan goes. Not only is your stay free, you're afforded an inside glimpse into each destination through your host. It's a cultural exchange. The hosts get to experience the world through their international guests, and the travelers are given a free place to crash, and local expertise. Each party leaves the arrangement with a new friendship from a different part of the world.

I've been active on CouchSurfing.org for a few years and have met some amazing people. When I first visited Thailand, my host introduced me to the expat community in Chiang Mai. A year later, I moved here.

Couchsurfing is easy and fairly safe. There's an optional verification process you can undergo to show others you're legit and dedicated to the community. After each stay, you and your host can leave positive or negative reviews that remain on your profile forever. The references weed out the dodgy people pretty quickly.

Your accommodations can have a huge range. With one host you could have your own room and bathroom and with another, you could share the floor with other couchsurfers. The description of the room/couch/floor available is located on the host's profile page. If you're flexible and open to sharing a space, you could meet some amazing hospitable folks (especially in Thailand). It's also a great way to get a sneak peak into expat life in any given city. I couchsurfed with teachers in Korea, Malaysia, and Vietnam and discovered which cities I would consider living and which cities were not well suited for me (Saigon being a big, busy no).

One thing to be mindful of while couchsurfing is outstaying your welcome. The number of days is usually arranged before you *surf* and the usual stay is between 2-3 nights. Some hosts are happy to let you extend your stay (in exchange for stocking their fridge or a nice gesture), but don't count on or expect it. I know one couch surfer who stayed in Chiang Mai for two months with his hosts – both Kiwis. They got on well and are now great friends.

Couchsurfing in a country as cheap as Thailand is mainly for the experience and to meet new people. Bear in mind, you might spend more on transport from your couch to the city than if you booked a room in the city centre (budget rooms can be found as cheaply as $3).

I have met people of all ages and walks of life while couchsurfing, so don't believe it's just for people in their early 20's. Many retirees with large homes decide to host because they enjoy the companionship, human connection, and sharing their passions with people from around the world.

In addition to accommodations , couchsurfing is also a community with groups, meet ups, and pre-arranged activities.

It's a great way to meet locals in a new city who can help you acclimate to your new expat life.

Read CouchSurfing 101[35] to learn more about the basics.

WORK EXCHANGE

Contrary to popular belief, the barter system is alive and well. Why not exchange your skills for room and board? When it comes to work exchanges, the person offering the room usually has a clear idea of what they need and want from you. That being said, be creative blending your skill-set with the business you'd like to work for. In Thailand, the work often includes gardening, farming, teaching English, writing, proofreading, business and marketing advice, and so on. There are more work opportunities available in Thailand than most other expat destinations. If you communicate your needs, there's usually a fair amount of flexibility with your job.

To search current work exchange opportunities check out the following websites:

Volunteer Work Thailand[36]

One of the most comprehensive work exchange / volunteer websites for Thailand. Almost all the opportunities listed are from established organizations. This website will link you to the organizations website where you can read more about the placement and email your questions and information directly.

---

35 http://bit.ly/couchsurfing101

36 http://bit.ly/volunteerthailand

Work Away[37]

A great website with an excellent diversity of work trades. Individuals, families, small business owners, and farmers place listings for work exchanges. After working a trade, you can rate the experience. This feature is great because it helps you choose your work exchange based on other volunteer's reviews. Some listings have a small fee to cover food or the costs of basic necessities like toilet paper. As of the writing of this book, there are 100 work exchange opportunities available in Thailand.

Helpx[38]

At the time of writing, Help.net had about 90 work exchange opportunities ranging from long-term needs like teaching to short term projects. One of the most interesting opportunities was translating a movie from English into Spanish as a video editor. In exchange for these skills, this particular job offered *"Your own house with kitchen right beside a lake and 200m from a paradise beach on the island of Koh Phangan"* to work from.

Wwoofing[39]

Wwoofing stands for *World Wide Opportunities for Organic Farming* and is an exchange program that offers the volunteer an opportunity to learn about perma-culture and organic farming skills. The website and the organization is well established and can put you in touch with farmers or gardeners needing extra help or wanting to spread perma-culture ideas to those interested. Hosts offer food and accommodations in exchange for your work on their property. This is one way to learn about food and fruits in Thailand.

---

[37] http://bit.ly/workawaythai

[38] http://bit.ly/helpxthailand

[39] http://bit.ly/wwoofthailand

If the thought of farming or teaching English doesn't appeal to you, not to worry. The idea of work for board is well known in Thailand and you can often design your own work exchange. Approach hotels or guest houses and offer to re-design their website in English, train the staff in the hotel about sales, offer marketing assistance, or take professional photos for them. The trick is to offer something that will improve their business at no cost to them. For best results, offer these exchanges during low season (Feb-Sept). Hotels are often too busy during high season to wheel and deal, nor do they have rooms available for barter (depending on the location).

The legality of work exchanges in Thailand varies depending on the type of work. Some longer term work exchanges offer a stipend, once you're getting paid for work that a Thai could clearly do, you have entered an immigration no-no. Working at a hotel reception or as a housekeeper are clearly jobs Thais could fulfill. Teaching English, web design, marketing, and other specialized skills fall in the acceptable range.

TIP
Work exchanges are a great way to learn some Thai. Hosts are always keen to teach you a few words. Come equipped with a <u>book for learning Thai</u> and you will find many people to help you study.

WORK HARD PLAY HARD

In Thailand, money talks

Thailand offers a wealth of opportunities if you know what to look for! Thailand attracts expats from all walks of life. In one bar you might meet a 70 year old expat Thai business owner and a 30 year old retiree! Many retirees open a restaurant or find work online and fit their work schedule around their free time. With so much free time, expats in Thailand have time to focus on their hobbies, exercise, learn a new language and sometimes even discover religion (many people take a meditation course at a Buddhist temple).

Another common occurrence when you decide to retire is having a new business idea that you've always wanted to do. Something you're genuinely interested in. If you're not ready to retire, it's relatively easy to find work. By far, the most common job for expats is teaching English. There's a constant demand for native English speakers to teach English or a range of other subjects in English. If you're not interested in teaching, then working in Thailand requires a bit more footwork and creativity.

You can start a location independent business selling a service or product. You could start an export business and sell unique Thai products in your home country, or work one of the hundreds of jobs available from your computer. This chapter will walk you through working and doing business in Thailand.

While there are many more work opportunities that aren't listed in this book, *Becoming an Expat* has a moral obligation to inform you about legal work opportunities, even though you may learn there are masses of expats who work illegally.

STARTING A BUSINESS

Before starting a business in Thailand, do your research. Starting a business in Thailand isn't for the faint of heart. Big business has a strong hold on many domestic markets, making it expensive to get into the game. Thai businesses have been a revolving door. You really have to understand your market. If your target audience is Thais, you need an advanced grasp of their culture.

Oftentimes, an easy market to breech is tourism, however, you need to provide something unique, or capitalize on a niche because the market is saturated in many regions.

That being said, Thailand has a lot of potential, particularly in online companies, manufacturing, and export businesses. The World Bank[40] ranks Thailand 91st out of 185 for difficulty starting a business, but for ease of doing business, it ranks high at 18th out of the same 185 countries. Getting in is tricky.

If you're determined to start a business in Thailand, you'll need to decide what type of company to set up.

---

[40] http://bit.ly/doingbusinessthai

EXPAT EXPERIENCE

Why did you start your own Business? What problems have you encountered doing business in Thailand over the years?

"When we first moved here, I worked for another TEFL company, but the opportunity came up to open my own TEFL school. Two years later, the perfect business partner arrived on Samui, which allowed me more free time for travel writing. I'm in charge of marketing and admin for Samui TEFL, and my partner, Kathryn, teaches the courses. My day is split between the school and my writing, a fulfilling combination for me.

The most difficult part of doing business here is the language barrier when dealing with paperwork and red tape. Also, it takes a while to get used to how everything works. However, with a good support team (accountant, lawyer, knowledgeable Thai and expat friends), you'll get into the rhythm of doing business in the land of smiles with a fair amount of ease. There seems to be a lot more paperwork in Samui than other regions. Hardly anything is done electronically, but it's a small price to pay for zero traffic, working and living on the island."

~ Rosanne Turner, www.samuiTEFL.com

HOW TO ORGANIZE

The first major question you need to ask yourself is, *"Do you want to create a Thai company (entice your Thai friends to become involved) or create a foreign-owned company?"*

THAI-OWNED

The easiest and most straightforward process is by incorporating a Thai-owned limited company. Thai limited companies must have 3 registered shareholders (at least one Thai) and a board of directors. Usually 51% is held by a Thai (either a wife, friend, or business partner) and if the company invests $62,500 they can issue a work permit for the foreign partner. If the foreigner is married to a Thai then the investment drops to about $30,000. Who said marriage wasn't a business arrangement? However, if you don't need the work permit and don't intend to actually work in the business (just manage it from your office), then the investment drops further to just $3,090.

TIP

Try to exceed the minimum financial investment required if you can. You need more flare! (Office Space reference) Providing the bare minimum raises red flags and your new company will be picked over with a fine-toothed comb. Try to add an additional 20-30% above the minimum investment.

Foreigners are allowed rights and can even **maintain full control of the company with 49%.** The majority Thai shares can be diluted so each has little control. When your Thai friends are the majority shareholders, your upfront investment is less. Whether you are organizing as a partnership or limited company, only 25% of the investment must be paid upfront.

FOREIGN-OWNED

If you want to set up a business with another foreigner, apply for a Foreign Business License (FBL) and request approval from the BOI (Board of Investment). In order to work in said business, you will need a work permit. In order to obtain this magical piece of paper, your company will need to have $62,500 in capital and employ four Thais who are each named in the Social Security system.

There is some wiggle room for additional work permits from the BOI if you'll be creating numerous jobs for Thais or if you're bringing new technology to the country. You should know, however, with the BOI you must *show them the money*! If you're investing the bare minimum, you likely won't even gain an audience with them.

This is why it's more common to start a Thai-owned limited company. If you can't get a foreign business license (or want an easier way), organizing as a Thai-owned company might be your best bet. The laws are complex regarding business registration, and with something so important, I would recommend seeking expert counsel.

After the company's Memorandum of Association (a document with all the business' shareholder information) is submitted, you can change the ownership section and transfer the shares to the foreigners involved. However, the shareholder divide must remain 51% Thai.

US TREATY OF AMITY

American citizens, or those who own American based businesses, who wish to conduct business in Thailand have it easier than other nationalities. This treaty allows American companies to hold majority shares (51% or more) and register as a shareholder from the get go.It also makes it possible for Americans to act as a sole proprietor, however, this doesn't provide them a work permit, so they still need to satisfy the minimum investment of $62,500 to earn one.

Do I really have to invest $62,500?

By far, the largest hurdle when starting a business in Thailand is the investment capital. Most people move to Thailand for the affordability, coming up with $62,500+ USD is no small feat. Which is exactly why the majority of folks decide to register as a *Thai Partnership* or *Thai Limited Company*.

There are instances (like retail sales) where the minimum investment is higher ($93,800). True to Thai standards, there are ways around that investment:

✦ If the foreigner is married to a Thai, the investment halves to $31,000

✦ A deal is struck with the BOI where special extenuating circumstances allow the rules to be adjusted

✦ Hire a company that specializes in obtaining work permits (potentially by utilizing illegal practices)

✦ Operate a foreign-registered online business and visit Thailand as a tourist, on a tourist visa

EMPLOYING THAIS

A Thai registered business must maintain the appropriate ratio of Thai to foreign staff. The first year is 2:1, each year thereafter is usually 4:1. If you can prove that Thais aren't capable of preforming the tasks your business requires, you could convince the BOI to approve addition foreign work permits throwing off the ratio. Language schools are one good example of a company that will not maintain a 4:1 ratio. Oftentimes, due to investment requirements, paperwork, and red tape required to secure proper work permits, companies such as language schools will ask their staff to work on tourist or education visas. We recommend you insist they obtain the appropriate work visa, even if you need to pay for the associated fees and do some of the leg work.

GETTING STARTED

The first step to your Thai based company is registering the prospective company name with the Department of Business Development.[41] The following steps can be done simultaneously: submit the Memorandum of Association (MOA), apply for the

---

establishment of the company, and submit your tax ID application. The process time will vary directly with the type of company you're attempting to establish. Best case scenario, filing the Memorandum of Registration can be accomplished in just one day provided all required documents are submitted.

✦ Find a trustworthy partner or shareholders for your business

✦ Find a permanent office (you will need the address to register the business)

✦ Choose a name and a logo – the logo you register will be transformed into a stamp that will go on all your future documents so choose it carefully

✦ File a *Memorandum of Association* to register your business and shareholders - You can register at the Commercial Registration Office but it's easier and stress free to have your lawyer take it from here. They will ensure all your paperwork is correct and translated into Thai

✦ Organize a few Thai staff members to register (ideally four Thai's to every foreigner involved). Maintenance and cleaning staff can be included

✦ Gather the company's documents in order to apply for a non-immigrant visa and work permit.

Thai Visa, a company specializing in assisting your visa needs, has an excellent website with a guide to apply for a work permit by yourself. [42]

While self education is important, I highly recommend you hire a reputable lawyer or specialist company to assist you through the process of starting a business. You're already dropping some serious coin in this venture, don't skimp where it counts. End game - it's worth the time you save. Registering the company is quite straightforward, working with immigration is another story.

---

[42] http://bit.ly/thaivisawork

TIP
Reputable companies that assist with business set up, visas, and work permits have excellent working relationships with Thai bureaucracy. You're not only paying for their expertise, your money is your ticket into a healthy relationship with bureaucracy. Which option is most affordable depends on how you value your time and stress.

Ask around in the expat community for a few referrals. Make sure the referring expat actually used the services of said attorney and didn't just hear they were good.

I spoke with business giant *Siam Legal* (www.siam-legal.com) who have offices across Thailand: Bangkok, Chiang Mai, Phuket, Pattaya, and have free international numbers to call from the US, UK or Australia. They have knowledgeable English speaking staff and can register and organize the paperwork for your business for around $940. You can also pay extra for them to organize the paperwork for a visa and work permit. Their website has a wealth of information about business in Thailand as well as laws you should acquaint yourself with, such as property and family law. My research also lead me to Sunbelt Legal Advisors (http://bit.ly/sunbeltthai).[43]

WORKING WITH THAIS

Welcome to a whole new work culture. In Thailand, there's a strong hierarchy. This means the boss' decision is final. If you work within a Thai company (or even a school), you'll observe the chain of command right away. Most people understand that foreigners have a different way of doing things, and they'll offer you a smile similar to one given to a child when you step out of

---

[43] http://bit.ly/sunbeltthai

cultural norms. However, if you're starting your own business here, prepare to practice your delegation skills and patience.

The official minimum wage in Thailand is $10 per *day*, or roughly $0.94 an hour. With such low wages, it's understandable why many Thais lack the motivation to work hard. You'll often see employees more focused on their smart phones than on customers (not too different from the US these days), and there's no such thing as *giving notice* when they've decided to move on to a different work venture. After payday, a staff member might not return. However, this isn't true for everyone. Some Thais perform above and beyond expectations in service and commitment to their job. Statistically, Thai female employees work harder than male employees. Maybe that's because of vast sexism (or cultural differences) in Thai business practices.

To keep staff happy, make certain your office/shop has air conditioning and an internet connection.

THAI TIME

If you're lucky, 9:00 am means sometime between 9 and 10 am. Buses, trains, and flights rarely leave on-time. The expectation is very much *"we'll get there when we get there"* so it's best if you can adapt and roll with the flow. Once you've been caught in a rainy season downpour, you'll understand the reason for Thai time. Would you rather arrive 20 minutes late or on-time and soaking wet?

TEACHING

Teaching English is by far the biggest expat job sector in Thailand. It's not the best paid but you're granted a liveable wage and a life in Thailand! To be highly marketable as a teacher, you should have a Bachelors degree (in anything) and a teaching certificate (TEFL, CELTA, TESOL). There are numerous companies in Thailand that offer the required certificate: TEFL- Teach English as a Foreign Language, TESOL- Teachers of English to Speakers of Other Languages, or CELTA- Certificate in English Language Teaching to Adults), housing, and a unique cultural experience all wrapped up into one package. Which is how many of the teachers end up in Thailand in the first place. I took a CELTA class and really enjoyed my training and experience.

All three certificates offer a classroom teaching experience and most companies also offer assistance finding jobs in Thailand after you complete the course. In Thailand, having one of these certificates makes you a teacher. For the rest of the world (and the international schools in Thailand), you barely have a foot in the classroom. In most countries, you're required to have a 1 year PGCE qualification, credentials, or have studied teaching as a degree.

For native English speakers with a four-year degree and a qualification (certificate listed above), you can turn up and secure a job in a week if you aren't picky. The government schools are always desperate for English speaking teachers to teach subjects like science or geography in English. The average government school will provide a work permit and pay $700-900 a month. In the smaller towns, they also provide housing. Private Thai schools usually pay a bit more but also expect more from their teachers. You might run into unhappy parents asking why their kids aren't already fluent.

Schools in Bangkok offer slightly higher salaries but the cost of living is also higher there so if you want to save money, look for jobs in smaller cities. If you aren't a native speaker but have near native English don't fear, most schools will be happy to hire you as well, so just keep asking around.

Attending a TEFL school that guarantees a job afterwards is the easiest way to find employment. If you don't have a degree it becomes trickier. Officially, Non-B visas and work permits can only be obtained if you have a Bachelor's degree, but for kindergartens or primary (Prathom) schools, the rules are more lax.

Thai Universities often hire English teachers for either the English Department or for the Language Department. They prefer to hire part-time or for set courses. A few of Bangkok's universities advertise online (on www.tefl.com) but for the most part, it's best to walk in, shake some hands, and leave a CV.

International schools are the best employers for teachers. They offer the best pay, will organize your visa paperwork for you, provide healthcare, and some offer to pay for your flights from your home country. In exchange, the international schools demand experienced and qualified teachers. The minimum they accept is a postgraduate certificate in education (PGCE), but most teachers they hire have a few years of experience under their belt as well.

When looking for teaching jobs in Thailand, the following sites have up-to-date listings:

✦Ajarn [44] – In Thailand only, ajarn.com lists both international and government jobs. The website also has good advice for new teachers.

✦TEFL [45] – has listings for teaching jobs worldwide but divides jobs by country.

✦Teach to Travel [46]- is actually a placement company but if you meet their requirements, they almost guarantee you a job. The pay is good and they offer assistance securing visas and getting to Thailand.

---

[44] ajarn.com

[45] www.tefl.com

[46] http://bit.ly/teachinthai

WORKING ONLINE

Working online is the second most popular expat job classification you'll observe in Thailand. Almost all online work is unofficial, although it might be someone's official job back home. All you need is a computer and an internet connection.

Your opportunities are only limited by your creativity. You can teach via Skype, buy and sell on Ebay, create a blog, website, or podcast and make money from the ad space, become a financial consultant, sell health food products, diet pills or dog food via a website you create, and more!

If you're not sure what you can do, check out elance (www.elance.com) or Odesk (www.odesk.com) for secure websites that match work to online freelancers. I have friends who have done some jobs on those sites, received good ratings for their work, and are now making a killing on specialized design projects.

If you're not sure what you want to do online, think about what you're good at or what you enjoy doing. Perhaps you have a business idea that you want to start to create. Or maybe you have the urge for a creative outlet such as making jewelry or clothing. Whatever it is that you have thought to yourself, *"wouldn't it be wonderful to have time to do____?"* see if you can create a business around ___. A great book to help you start your virtual life is Tim Ferris's 4 Hour Work Week.[47] He offers a new way to look at work, and introduces you to the concept of working for yourself.

TELECOMMUTE

Telecommuting is similar to working online but with the assumption that you already have a job. Most jobs these days

---

[47] http://bit.ly/4hrworkweekbook

require a computer, an internet connection, and a few words between co-workers. If you work in an office, think about your job – could you do it from home? What aspect of your job keeps you in an office? Could you communicate with your colleagues and boss via Skype or email?

More and more people are working from home. Zero commute, flexible working hours, favorable work environment, less overhead for employers, it's an all around win-win. Studies have shown employees are more productive when they can set their own schedule.

The first step is to find out if your company has a telecommuting program. If not, then you will have some convincing to do. You'll want to consider any requirements your employer has before you pitch the idea to them. Read Remote: Office Not Required,[48] the book will help you make your pitch rock solid. Agree on a probation period to prove yourself as an independent worker.

If your boss refuses to let you work out of the office, maybe it's time to consider what other jobs you can do with your skill set.

INDEPENDENT CONSULTANT

Your years of experience don't have to disappear once you move abroad. Why not bundle up your experience and become an independent consultant? You could consult in – nutrition, fitness, business, marketing, design, IT, security, fashion, counseling, education, life coaching, social media, or multi-media.

The trick is to find your niche. Start a simple wordpress website (or find someone on www.Odesk.com to make one for you) and reach out to your network. Offer heavy discounts or free trials to debug your new business and gain a happy referral base.

---

[48] http://bit.ly/remoteoffice

Depending on your business, you could target markets around the world.

PROPERTY MANAGEMENT/ REAL ESTATE

Bangkok and Samui have the largest expat real estate management markets. As the number of expats and retirees continue to increase in cities like Phuket and Chiang Mai, there will be a great need for knowledgeable real estate agents and property managers. Since the property laws allow foreigners to legally own condominiums, there's a huge market in apartments.

An average one bedroom condominium in Phuket sells for $50,000. You don't need a real estate license in Thailand, which means you can jump right in. Make sure to read up on property laws and all things one would be required to learn if there were a required license. You want to do your clients justice after all.

Agents need their own car to take clients to showings and should have a superb grasp of their region and market. If you already have a US license and a track record for the luxury market you might be able to jump straight into selling high end apartments.

The trick to finding work with a real estate company is by offering them something they don't already have – be it experience, ability to advertise, a foreign language, or a proven sales record.

TOURISM JOBS

The tourism market is both difficult to enter and potentially lucrative. The most important thing to consider in tourism is are you doing a job that could be done by a Thai person – if the answer is yes, you won't be able to get a work permit or work legally. If no, then the country will welcome you with open arms since you will bring in more money for the industry. You can start your own tourism business catering to a certain niche (i.e. adventure sports, retirees, family travel, gay travel), work as a tour guide (especially with various languages), a hotel manager, or quality assessor. If you previously worked with an international hotel chain, it's possible to relocate to Bangkok or other large city. If you have a way of bringing people to Thailand that Thai's don't (e.g. for study tours or holidays), you can set yourself up as a company (based in either your home country or Thailand) and get a visa and work permit through said company.

NGO's, NON-PROFITS & VOLUNTEERING

The NGO (Non Governmental Organization) sector is a huge source for expat employment. Jobs in this sector come in all shapes and sizes including: accountants, project managers, logistics and training coordinators, language or vocational skill trainers, and doctors or nurses. The international organizations such as United Nations, Red Cross or Medecinas sans frontieres pay very good Western salaries but are very competitive. The smaller NGOs will usually pay a local wage but sometimes supply basic housing and food. UN Jobs (www.unjobs.org) advertise most NGO job vacancies in Thailand. For smaller NGO opportunities Idealist (www.idealist.org)would be more down your alley.

There are numerous volunteer opportunities in Thailand. You can offer your skills, time, and sweat. It's that simple. If you volunteer over 12 hours a week and the organization is registered in Thailand, they can arrange a volunteer visa (non- O) for you.

SPORTS EXERCISE & YOGA

If you're fit and passionate about fitness, you could make a business out of it. Yoga and scuba diving are huge in Thailand, especially in the high season (Nov-Jan) when tourist flood Thailand. Specialized sports trainers are likely to find jobs that come with work visas. Most coaching jobs are based in Bangkok. Gyms, weightlifting, and other sports like CrossFit are increasing in popularity but require you to set up your own company (or find an umbrella company to open it under).

EXPAT EXPERIENCE

"I originally came to Thailand to learn to be a Divemaster. After I completed my training, I had fallen so in love with Thailand that I didn't want to leave.

I got a job as a mermaid performer and underwater model/stunt actress. I'd always wanted to be The Little Mermaid as a child and I thought scuba diving was as close as I could get, until I discovered 'Mermaiding.' Using a Monofin for freediving and a tail cover, I perform underwater and on land for a variety of occasions. It's a great job but it requires a lot of hard work and training. I've improved my breath holding skills to over 3 minutes, and I'm now a competitive free-diver. Working in Thailand has given me so many opportunities to try new things and be adventurous. I would never have thought I would become a real life mermaid."

~ Melanie Long, Mermaid Melanie, Phuket

MISC. JOBS

In Bangkok there are jobs in: banking, education, retail, manufacturing, and most multinational companies are able to hire foreigners – especially if you have a transferable job like accountant or project manager. Some multinational companies hire staff from abroad, making it possible to secure a job before even arriving. <u>Check Career Jet</u> (<u>www.careerjet.co.th</u>) or <u>Jobs DB</u> (<u>http://th.jobsdb.com/th</u>).

WORK VISAS AND PERMITS

In order to legally work in Thailand, you'll need a work permit which is valid for one year. This is obtained through your employer. To get a work permit you'll need to already be in possession of a non-immigrant visa (non-b type or a non-o) valid for at least 90 days. It takes the labor office 3 to 6 weeks to process permits. When you finally get the work permit, your company will keep it safe for you. It's important to get copies of it because immigration occasionally wants to see the copy to prove you are, indeed, working. More importantly, showing a work permit at national parks and popular tourists destinations gets you the Thai price $0.63, instead of tourist price $6.30.

VIRTUAL OFFICE 101

Now that your office is virtual, you can design it however you want. Where do you work best? What time of day are you most productive? Do you work best while alone or surrounded by people? Do you want coffee on tap?

In your first few months working location independently, you'll learn a lot about what's best for you and your ideal work environment. Personally, I wrote most of this book at home. In cafes, the people distract me too much (I love to people watch). I'm also not really focused in the afternoons, so I try to work early in the mornings or in the evenings. Once I realized that afternoons were not for work, I began to wonder how many wasted afternoons I'd spent in an office starting at a screen pretending/attempting to work. Luckily, that's in the past. Now I can work wherever and whenever I want.

COMMUNICATION

The top two resources for international communication are Skype and magicJack. My personal preference is Skype but I've seen many happy magicJack customers as well.

With Skype, you can buy a US or Canadian number for $60 USD per year that will allow customers or co-workers to ring your Thai phone as long as your Skype app is open and you have a solid network connection (be it 3G or wifi). You can also purchase unlimited calling to the US & Canada, starting at just $4.99 USD per month. Skype also offers unlimited world monthly packages that allow you to call landlines and mobiles in: Thailand, the US, Singapore, Hong Kong, and Canada starting at $13.99 USD.

INTERNET

Consistent internet is vital if you plan on working online. In Thailand, it is easy to find internet access but a bit harder to find speedy internet. Scout out the providers in your area. Talk to your neighbors and see who is happy with their service. Perform speed tests on the local wifi hotspots. Consider signing up for the provider who has the best local hotspot wifi speed and availability in your area. That way, you will be connected at home and can be connected in local hotspots across the city. See *Communications* in the *Logistics* section for more information about internet and data. Thailand's cafes are always a good fall back if you need fast internet. In the bigger cities they are open late, and Bangkok and Chiang Mai have a few 24 hour internet cafes that can double as your late night office.

GET ORGANIZED

If you're working for various time zones, add the corresponding clocks to your computer. Google calendar is a free and amazingly convenient tool. You can add all important deadlines, conference calls, and events. A key feature is it automatically syncs with your smartphone (as long as you've loaded your gmail account on the device). You can set alarms, reminders, and email alerts. There are also thousands of free 'to do list' apps available. I use Google Keep [49] which lets you write notes, set reminders and create tick lists.

VIRTUAL ADMIN SUPPORT

If you need help managing day to day tasks so you can fill your time doing what you do best, consider hiring a part-time secretary. Labor is very affordable in Thailand, running around $10 a day. However, if you aren't set up as a Thai business, you will need to look into hiring a virtual assistant (VA). It may sound cooky to you, but virtual assistants have been around for awhile now. They're simply admin staff who work remotely, like you. There are a couple of paths you can take when searching for the right VA. You can place an ad on career sites or you can query VA staffing companies such as ReceptionHQ.com. They advertise that their experienced VAs start part-time for just $49 per month (plus an additional $1.20 per call).

Common tasks include organizing your appointments and calendar, taking your calls, answering frequently asked questions, and assisting with social media management. ReceptionHQ is another service to look into. Ironically, if your company is registered in the US or Europe, you can hire a Thai call center to

---

handle your customer support. They operate in English, Spanish, German, French and Russian.

ONLINE BANKING

Before you come to Thailand you should evaluate your current bank and test it for international compatibility. See **Banking** in the **Before You Arrive** section. Make sure you can wire money, bill pay, transfer money between banks, utilize Paypal, and aren't charged currency transaction or ATM fees.

TIP
In Thailand, online banking is offered for personal accounts but not for business accounts.

MERCHANT ACCOUNTS

If you will be accepting credit card payments internationally, you'll need a merchant account and a mobile card reader. Paypal offers a free merchant account and is easy to integrate into your website. It's also one of the most recognized methods of online payment. However, Paypal charges a 2.7% commission on each purchase. The Square[50] was recommended to me by a few different *digital nomads* in Thailand. It's user friendly and is also free to set up. However, they charge a higher commission at 2.75% per transaction.

MOVING MONEY

Western Union

An oldie but goodie at times. Western Union cuts out the middle man and allows you to send money to people around the world.

Wire Transfer

This is the most used and simplest way to send larger sums of money into the country. Unfortunately, times are changing. The assumption is (from the US government), if you're moving large sums of money out of the US, then you must be doing something naughty with it. Since FACTA[51] passed, banks are required to ask you what you're doing with *your* money as if that's any of their business!

---

[50] http://bit.ly/squarethai

[51] http://www.irs.gov/Businesses/Corporations/Foreign-Account-Tax-Compliance-Act-FATCA

Paypal

Paypal can be a great way to get paid for a service or product. You must link your Paypal account to a US bank account to gain access to all of its features. So, if you're looking for a US-free financial solution, this isn't it.

Wells Fargo

Wells Fargo has an option called "Express Send." You can wire money online from your US account to your account in Thailand (specific participating banks) for just $9. Not only is it a great rate but it's called express for a reason, it arrives in less than an hour. In order to set up *Express Send,* you must go through a two week set up process but it's worth it! They also have an account package called the PMA package[52] that allows you two fee-free ATM withdrawals per statement period. The PMA package has a $30 monthly fee that is waived if you maintain at least $25,000 in your account.

If you send money to a Thai Bank that's not on their "special list," they charge the industry standard $40-$50.

MAIL

Getting your mail can be interesting while abroad. Despite the excellent Thai postal system, you'll need a home address for credit cards, government paperwork, and for your business if it's registered abroad. The easiest method is to use a family member or best friend's address or mail service. See *Mail* in the *Before You Arrive* section for more details.

The most popular international mail providers for Thailand are:

---

[52] http://bit.ly/fargoPMA

Mailboxes etc - www.mbe.com
Mailboxes Thailand - www.mbethai.com/mbe_network.asp
USAmail1- www.usamail1.com
UK Postbox – www.ukpostbox.com
US Global Mail - www.usglobalmail.com
Aeropost – www.aeropost.com
My US - www.MyUS.com

ELECTRONICS

If you're going to be location independent, your electronics will play a huge role. You'll need a laptop, back up device, Skype or magicJack capable phone, and an unlocked smartphone to start. Depending on your type of work, it might be worthwhile to invest in a larger external monitor, mouse and keyboard. See *Electronics* in the *Before You Arrive* section for more information.

PAYING THE MAN

Tax isn't often a favorite subject, but we're all required to face the beast or hire someone else to face the beast and report back. The good news for expats working in Thailand is Thai taxes are fairly straightforward and accountants are cheap! Keep in mind I'm not a tax professional, and this section is not designed to be your only tax reference.

THAI TAXES -*individuals*

Thai tax works on a progressive scale. Here are the tax rates of the Personal Income Tax:

Taxable Annual Income (USD)	Tax Rate (%)
$4,690	0
more than $9,380	5
more than $15,640	10
more than $23,460	15

Taxable Annual Income (USD)	Tax Rate (%)
more than $31,280	20
more than $62,560	25
more than $125,120	30
+$125,120	35

*Source: revenue department

DEDUCTIONS

You're not taxed for any income that's less than $1,875. You can also claim a personal deduction of $940 for yourself. If you're married and your spouse isn't working, you get another $940 deduction. If you have children, you can claim $470 each for up to three children ($530 each if they are studying in Thailand).

Now the fun begins. There are two types of taxes for individuals – residents and non-residents. Thailand's Revenue department make the distinction as follows:

"Taxpayers are classified into resident and non-resident. "Resident" means any person residing in Thailand for a period or periods aggregating more than 180 days in any tax (calendar) year. A resident of Thailand is liable to pay tax on income from sources in Thailand as well as on the portion of income from foreign sources that is brought into Thailand. A non-resident is, however, subject to tax only on income from sources in Thailand."

In many cases, your employer will help organize your taxes for you. While I've never heard of expats having tax troubles, I would recommend hiring a reputable accountant to keep up with all requirements. With a work permit, you'll get a tax code that you'll need to file. The tax year runs from January 1st to December 31.st

Ask your accountant about the taxation of your income from a foreign source. The unspoken rule for expats in Thailand is *money earned abroad should be kept abroad*. Just because your new life is in Thailand doesn't mean you should close your bank account and move your money here. It's better to keep your money abroad (in case of exchange rate fluctuations) and withdraw money from the bank or ATM when you need it.

Many countries have signed tax treaties with Thailand to avoid individuals paying tax twice on the same income including: the US, UK, Australia, France, and New Zealand. However, don't just rely on the treaty. Fill out the necessary forms and provide evidence that you are living in Thailand to ensure that your home country is satisfied.

THAI TAXES - *corporation*

Corporate taxes for Thai businesses are based on worldwide income. Foreign businesses operating in Thailand only pay tax on profit earned in Thailand. At the time of writing, the corporate tax rate was 30% but there are special reductions for small businesses (meaning a business with less than $156,400 capital at the end of the accounting year).

✦ Companies with a net profit of up to $30,800 – 15% tax
✦ Companies with a net profit over $30,900 – 23% tax (until 2015, then 25%)
✦ Companies with a net profit over $92,700 – 30% tax

Businesses need to submit a semi-annual tax return (CIT 51 form) after the first 6 months and an annual tax return (CIT 50 form) 150 days after the closing date of its accounting period, along with payment. It's recommended to hire a Thai accountant to fill out these forms out in Thai as they are complex and mistakes could be problematic to the running of your business.

For more information see Thailand's Revenue Department website[53]

ACCOUNTING IN THAILAND

The average accountant will charge less than $63, to fill out and file your Thai tax forms for you.

US TAXES

It doesn't take a tax professional to recognize that the US wants their cut of the pie. Some expats have given up their citizenship in an effort to avoid paying taxes to a country they do not live in. If your worth is greater than $622,000 and you gave up your citizenship, you may be pursued by the IRS for tax evasion. The US has even gone so far as to create an Expatriation Tax which requires the expat who has renounced their citizenship to pay taxes for 10 years after they are no longer a US citizen.

Since the US is losing people from the highest tax brackets to other countries, they have enacted a new law to deter others from emigrating. You are no longer allowed to reacquire your citizenship once you renounce it. Seems like the government holds a grudge.

FATCA- *Foreign Account Tax Compliance Act*[54]

---

[53] http://bit.ly/thaiIRS

[54] To read the argument why FATCA is bad for America go to: http://bit.ly/FATCAbad

FATCA is a government response to heavyweight tax evaders. A provision as recent as July 1, 2014 was initiated through FATCA *requiring* foreign financial institutions with US clients to provide annual reports to the IRS with the name, address, largest account balance in the year, and total debits and credits of any account owned by their U.S. customer. The new law is a way for the United States to monitor where you are, how much money you have, and impose a 30% withholding tax for institutions holding US securities who do not comply.

It's going to be a roller coaster ride watching this dramatic new law play out. Only time will tell how big of a mess we'll end up in. Hundreds of international banks have closed the accounts of their US customers due to the outrageous demands by the US (FATCA).

You can file your US tax return through a US Embassy or mail it.[55]

FOREIGN EARNED INCOME EXCLUSION
for US citizens

A potential break in the aggressive US tax requirements is the Foreign Earned Income Exclusion. In order to qualify, you must be a US citizen, your tax country must be outside of the US, be a "bona fide resident" of Thailand *(or other non-US country)*, and have spent ≥330 full days there during a period of 12 consecutive months. The days are in total, they do not have to be consecutive, and are not reset on January 1st. In any 12 month span, you cannot have spent more than 34 days outside of Thailand to qualify.

If you qualify, you won't have to pay any taxes on income up to $97,600. You may also qualify to deduct foreign housing costs. The

---

[55] Go to the IRS website, U.S. Citizens and Resident Aliens Abroad section for more information.

annual cap for the housing exclusion is $29,280 or 30% of the maximum Foreign Earned Income Exclusion. Remodeling, decorating, and furnishing is not included.

If you qualify for the exclusion, it doesn't mean you don't have to file taxes. You are required to file if you made more than $9,750 in world-wide income. You may not pay a dime, but Uncle Sam wants to keep an eye on you.

The most popular tax forms for the expat are the standard 1040, Form 2555-Foreign Earned Income Exclusion and the Form 1116- Foreign Tax credit.

The rules for this exclusion are not simple. I would recommend using a CPA or other tax professional who specializes in expatriate taxes. This section is in no way to be used as the sole reference for tax guidance. It's simply a farang's take on expat taxes as best I can understand.

FBAR
Report of Foreign Bank & Financial Accounts [56]

Any US citizen that has over $10,000 in accumulative accounts outside of the US at anytime during the calendar year is required to report it to the US government. Even if it was for the purchase of a house, and you simply transferred the money into your Thai bank account where it was immediately routed out during escrow.

The filing deadline is June 30th every year. This year (2014) was the first time it was required to file online. You will need to download free Adobe Acrobat if your computer doesn't already have it.

---

[56] http://bit.ly/FBARtax

CANADIAN TAX CONSIDERATIONS[57]

If you're Canadian and planning a move to Thailand, the government requests that you inform the Canada Revenue Agency (CRA) before you leave to work out your residency status. They have a form to help you decide what status fits your situation: NR73. Numerous Canadian expats feel that they can decide what their residency status is for themselves and opt not to share information.

In order to keep your GSI (Guaranteed Income Supplement), you need to prove that you are in Canada for six months of the year. Below is a list of other deal breakers that would result in the loss of your GSI:

◆ You don't file an individual Income Tax and Benefit Return by April 30, or if, by the end of June each year, they have not received the information about your net income for the previous year
◆ You leave Canada for more than six consecutive months
◆ Your net income is above the maximum annual[58] income
◆ You are incarcerated in a federal penitentiary for two years or longer
◆ You die (morbid but true)

I always advise you to consult your tax professional with important decisions such as this one. Reading through governmental jargon is seemingly impossible to decipher. So if the below bullet-points leave you scratching your head or throwing this book across the room, just leave it to the professionals.

The information below covers each resident status in Canada and is quoted from a Canadian governmental website: travel.gc.ca

---

[57] http://bit.ly/CanuckImmigration

[58] http://bit.ly/maxlimit

✦**Factual residents**
  · Working temporarily outside Canada
  · Teaching or attending school in another country
  · Commuting (going back and forth daily or weekly) from Canada to your place of work in the United States, or
  · Vacationing outside Canada

✦**Deemed residents**
  · A federal, provincial or territorial government employee who was a resident of Canada just before being posted abroad or who received a representation allowance for the year
  · A member of the Canadian Forces
  · A member of the Canadian Forces oversea's school staff who chooses to file a return as a resident of Canada
  · Working under a Canada International Development Agency assistance program if you were a resident of Canada at any time during the three-month period just before you began your duties abroad
  · A dependent child of one of the four persons described above and your net income for the year was not more than the basic personal amount (line 300 in the General Income Tax and Benefit Guide) or
  · A person who, under an agreement or convention (including a tax treaty) between Canada and another country, is exempt from tax in that other country on 90% or more of their income from all sources because of their relationship to a resident (including a deemed resident) of Canada

✦**Non-residents**
  · Normally or routinely live in another country and are not considered a resident of Canada
  · Do not have significant residential ties to Canada, and
  · Live outside Canada throughout the tax year, or

· Stay in Canada for less than 183 days in the tax year

✦**Deemed non-residents**
  · If you are a factual resident or a deemed resident of Canada and are considered to be a resident of another country that has a tax treaty with Canada, you may be considered a deemed non-resident of Canada for income tax purposes.

BRITISH PENSIONS

QROPS & QNUPS[59] are two five letter acronyms every British expat should know.

QROPS stands for Qualifying Recognized Overseas Pension Scheme, but is often called an 'offshore' pension because the providers of said pension work from financial centers around the world.

There are more than 3,000 options available across 46 countries. Some expats opt to work with a financial adviser instead of dealing directly with a QROPS provider. There are various rules and tax implications depending on the laws of the country where the program is based.

Reasons why a Brit might want to consider a QROPS include:
✦Up to 30% lump sum availability
✦Inherent tax free
✦Portability

QNUPS stands for Qualifying Non-UK Pension Scheme. The two programs are very similar, consult your financial advisor to decide which is better for you and your family.

---

[59] http://bit.ly/UKexpatpension

INTERNATIONAL TAX

There are a variety of proposals being thrown around worldwide to create an international tax or tax on a company/individual's worldwide income. The provocation for change is international multi-million dollar companies including Google, Starbucks, and rich individuals who have given up their US citizenship just before receiving a large sum of money from an investment or inheritance while utilizing international shields to dodge paying taxes (hello Eduardo Saverin).

The United States and other developed countries have realized that without the proper taxation of these mega offshore companies and rich individuals, they are losing billions of dollars. Other people argue it's simply a matter of control. Whatever your belief, changes will likely be on the way in the next few years.

In 2013, the US saw more than double the number of people emigrating than any other full year in the history of the United States, over 3,000 people. This shift is believed due to a 2010 law entitled the Foreign Account Tax Compliance Act (FATCA) which was implemented this year (2014). The FATCA makes it 'legal' for the US to bully financial institutions around the world into providing account numbers of clients who hold US citizenship. This information is then sent to the good ole' IRS. Read more about FATCA in the *US Tax* section.

As of this writing, there are no taxes on worldwide income. By definition, an international tax would create double taxation. If the US is successful in creating it, they will be able to add double taxation to Washington D.C.'s taxation without representation faux pa. Keep your eye on this issue if you own an international business or have assets in a foreign bank.

BUSINESS BANKING

To open a business account you'll need your passport, business' Memorandum of Association, a copy of the shareholder list, a copy of the company certificate with company stamp (if any) issued by a registrar within the previous 30 days, meeting minutes resolving to approve account opening with SCB (or other bank) and the VAT registration certificate. Bank branches vary so if one won't open an account for you, head to the next branch and see if they would like your business.

Make sure you open your business account close to your office address because as mentioned earlier, business accounts don't offer online banking so you will need to enter the bank, sign and stamp every transaction.

HEALTHCARE

The low down on healthcare and why there are so many hospitals

Health is what you make of it. Half the expats in Thailand are healthier than they were in their home country (thanks to fresh fruit and yoga). The other half are drinking way too much beer, driving their motorbikes too fast, and taking daily advantage of cheap steaks and fried chicken. No matter how good you care for yourself, there's always a chance you will need to seek medical attention at some point during your stay in Thailand.

PREVENTION

The land of fresh fruit and sunshine is ideal for improving one's health. On the surface, Thai people look slim and healthy. However, the younger generation don't exercise and eat vast amounts of sugar and processed meats.

- ✦ Eat a traditional Thai diet - Rice and vegetables with a little meat. Check out the yellow bannered vegetarian restaurants.
- ✦ Snack on fresh fruit and replace sugary drinks with fresh fruit smoothies or coconuts.

✦ Practice your Thai! Mai sai nam dtaan or mai waan will stop them from putting sugar or syrup in your drinks.
✦ Walk daily – Explore the local area, walk to the market for breakfast or along the beach every sunset.
✦ Meditate – join a meditation circle or take a course at the monastery. It's a great stress reducing activity.

CARE

One of the biggest concerns for an expat is access to good affordable healthcare. Moving to Thailand provides you access to a range of great healthcare options. There are numerous doctors and dental clinics scattered across the country but they vary greatly in quality of care. Expat referrals are key to finding a competent doctor. It's also a great application of the Facebook forums (see directory for a list of groups to get you started).

If you don't know where to begin your hunt, most hospitals also have clinics inside. It's best to call and book an appointment. Thai clinics have a reputation for being clean, sterile, and usually decorated in a pastel color.

Many big city doctors have received at least part of their education abroad (see their certificates hanging proudly on their walls) and generally speak intermediate or advanced English. However, doctors here don't like explaining their diagnosis which can cause a bit of a culture clash. In Thailand, the doctor is the higher authority, so the patient should respect his word vs. the Western mentality of not treating him as god and taking responsibility for your own body. This is not to say you aren't permitted to ask questions, just tread lightly and ask politely.

Thailand ranks first place for the cheapest healthcare according to the Bloomberg's Efficiency Table. It also ranks higher than the US for efficiency and cost per capita. The two most efficient healthcare systems (Hong Kong and Singapore) are also daily direct flights from Bangkok.

> **TIP**
>
> Ambulances here don't work the way they do in other countries. If you're lucky enough to be picked up by an ambulance, you'll probably spend longer in traffic than if you were on the back of a motorbike. If you have any condition that may need immediate attention at a hospital (e.g. cardiac history), then it's wise to find an apartment not too far from a good hospital and your cardiologist.

HOSPITALS

Hospitals in Thailand have many different levels and are distinguished by cost and quality of care. In big cities, there are at least three or four hospitals to choose from. The private hospitals are more expensive but often provide better care than the government-owned hospitals whose interiors are bare, grey and nothing has been updated since it opened. Government owned hospitals also have longer wait times without appointments. If you need a consultation with a specialist, find out when they are going to be in the government hospital – it will work out much cheaper.

There are mid-range hospitals that offer the best value for your money. Good quality service without extra charges (like a mini kitchen in your private room). Ask around for the mid-range hospital with the best reputation. Seasoned expats (or Thaivisa.com's forums) will be able to advise you.

Finally, there are the 5 star hotels, I mean hospitals. They offer the best service and equipment (with the same doctors as the government hospital). Prices for all treatments and medicines are double that of the government hospital. Most of their patients are covered by private insurance and aren't paying out of pocket so they don't care about the costs and would rather have the 5 star treatment.

It pays (or should I say saves) to know which hospitals are pricey! <u>Bumrungrad International Hospital</u>[60] is one of Bangkok's highest rated hospitals with state of the art equipment and internationally qualified doctors. However, it's also the most expensive in the country with a night's stay running $250, compared to the standard $93, price found elsewhere. They even have *Royal suite rooms* – book one of these and you may forget you're even sick!

In all three types of hospitals there will be English speaking staff. The staff recognizes you are a foreigner and will immediately find a staff member who can translate or assist you. Most doctors speak decent English.

EXPAT EXPERIENCE

"I get basic health insurance coverage through my work. The international hospitals are generally very good and the staff speaks decent English. I've had to go to the hospital a few times over the years and I've never had issues. If you have major health problems, you should research the best hospitals in the area you'd like to live. Local clinics and pharmacies are a bit of a joke as far a diagnosing health issues. For anything serious, I would recommend you head to an international hospital."

~ **Julie** Cousineau, Primary school teacher

THAI INSURANCE - *The basics that come with your job*

If you're working in Thailand, you will likely be provided with the government-run Social Security Insurance (SSI). It provides free basic care in smaller government-owned hospitals. It might not live up to the standard of care you prefer. Government hospitals are known for long waits and shared exam rooms (where everyone stares at the *farang*). SSI is certainly better than

---

[60] http://bit.ly/thaihospital

nothing, but leaves much to be desired. SSI doesn't cover preventative care such as doctor visits or medications.

PRIVATE INSURANCE

Many expats spring for private health insurance. This provides peace of mind and often a high standard of care in Thailand. The annual expense can range from $500-1,700 per year depending on insurance company, age, medical condition, and add ons. Make sure and get at least four or five quotes before selecting your insurance. If you are considering international companies, like Bupa, cost compare Bupa International to Bupa Thailand. You are likely to find the local chapter offers the best rates.

Speaking of Bupa, they are the most common and well known insurer in Thailand amongst expats. They have a plan for everyone. You can purchase a Thailand only plan or upgrade to worldwide coverage (excluding USA & Canada).

Beyond Personal Care Plan[61] including personal accident coverage starts at $780. Even their Platinum plan starts at just $1,000, based on a 45 year old American with an office job.

TIP
If you decide not to include "out-patient benefits" in your insurance plan, it suddenly becomes a chunk cheaper. Out patient benefits are things like doctors consultations and prescribed drugs, x- rays, screenings and tests. Unless you are a hypochondriac, you can save quite a bit of money by paying the out patient things yourself.

---

[61] http://bit.ly/bupaplan

Another recommended insurer is <u>A Plus International</u>.[62] They offer personal plans covering hospital stays and treatments starting at $1,000 USD annually.

Allianz, AXA, Aviva, and Aetna also cover expats in Thailand but their plans were quoted as $1,500, $2,100, $1,900 and $1,700 respectively. There are numerous companies in the USA and Europe that will insure you for Thailand and if you already have a good insurer, email them to see if Thailand is covered.

If you are insuring a couple or family, per person prices become cheaper than those quoted above.

Things to consider before purchasing insurance:

✦Am I covered worldwide (incl. or excluding USA) or only in Thailand?
✦How much of hospital stays and surgery does the plan cover?
✦Do I *need* out patient benefits?
✦Does it include emergency repatriation?
✦Does it cover cancer, HIV, and other treatments?
✦What am I responsible to pay (deductible)?
✦What hospitals are included in the insurance?

PAYING OUT OF POCKET

There are quite a few expats living in Thailand who don't have insurance. They are often young or healthy and figure the cost of healthcare is affordable so they opt to pay for their needs as they occur. Many other expats believe the peace of mind insurance gives them is well worth the upfront expense and potential savings in the long run. If you decide to opt out of health insurance, make sure you save an *emergency health fund,* just in case.

---

[62] http://bit.ly/Aplusinsurance

Average Cost	Government hosp - Private hosp $USD
A night at a hospital	$60 - $250
Consultation with a doctor	$3 - $15
Antibiotics	$3 – $30 (always buy them in pharmacies not the hospital)
Emergency surgery	$30 - $300
Rabies shots (for humans)	$25 – $100

TRAVEL INSURANCE

If you're planning on living in Thailand part-time, you should cost compare travel insurance against health insurance. Travel insurance usually covers health emergencies, hospital stays, and emergency evacuation. If often also includes reimbursement for flight cancellations/delays due to weather and lost luggage. Travel insurance can be purchased per day. If you plan to ride elephants or a motorbike, go scuba diving, or other adventurous activities, you should buy extra insurance to cover your more daring days.

There are many companies that offer reasonable travel insurance but one that is often highly recommended is World Nomads.[63] They offer extremely competitive rates and include emergency evacuations in all their plans. A 12 month basic coverage for an American under 70 was quoted at $1,050. This includes worldwide (excluding the US) emergency coverage, which is great for those who plan to explore neighboring Asian countries.

---

[63] http://bit.ly/worldnomadsinsurance

THREATS TO YOUR HEALTH

The Roads – Logic and rules don't always apply while driving in Thailand. Couple that with the learning curve to drive a motorbike plus throw in a beer or two and you're heading for disaster. Many expats experience a motorbike accident. Often it's as simple as a burning hot exhaust pipe against your leg (your Thai tattoo).

Malaria and Dengue Fever – two scary diseases carried by mosquitoes. The carriers are usually found in the jungle and border areas but occasionally you'll hear of a case in the city. Both require bed rest, medication, and time. If you catch either disease a second time, your effects are doubled. Buy mosquito repellent spray and keep it in your bag. Sleep with mosquito nets and spray your clothes with deet[64] when you're in the jungle.

HIV- Thailand has a rising rate of HIV so make sure and practice safe sex. It's easy to get tested in Bangkok but outside of the capital it becomes harder to find testing clinics.

Rabies – Rabies is alive and well in Thailand. So if you're bit by a dog, it's recommended you go to the nearest hospital for a rabies shot. Some people act preemptively and get the vaccination before they arrive in Thailand. Speaking of vaccinations…

VACCINATIONS

Plan on getting slightly perforated before coming to Thailand. If you prefer, you can wait and get them done here. You'll need the following injections: Japanese encephalitis, typhoid, tetanus, Hepatitis A and B, and rabies if you'd like.

---

[64] http://bit.ly/deet4clothes

PHARMACIES (*YA- in Thai*)

In big cities pharmacies can be found everywhere. Drugs are cheap and you can buy most things over the counter. Usually the staff will be able to speak English and advise you on your symptoms. In Thai, the words for most medicines are the same as in English. Paracetamol, antibiotics, mosquito sprays, condoms, tampons, bandages, birth control pills, anti diarrhea tablets are all available for about the same cost (or less) than in the States. Pharmacies are called Ya (which means drug in Thai) and some are even open 24 hours. 7-Elevens also carry basic medical supplies such as aspirin.

MEDICAL TOURISM

Medical tourism is becoming more popular worldwide as health costs rise and government waiting lists lengthen. Bangkok is a medical tourism hotspot, specifically for dentistry and minor surgeries. People flock from around the world to take advantage of the affordable high quality Thai healthcare. Thailand's tourism board has created a specialized medical tourism guide on <u>their website</u>.[65] Their <u>international patient guide</u>[66] is useful for tourists and expats alike. It guides you through choosing a hospital, making an appointment, locating a doctor, and after treatment care. They offer a handy list of questions to ask your doctor including:

◆What qualifications do you hold and where did you receive them?

---

[65] <u>http://bit.ly/medicaltourismthai</u>

[66] <u>http://bit.ly/thaiptguide</u>

✦Are you certified with local, national, and/or international
  health organizations?

✦What training have you received for performing this procedure?

✦How many operations like this have you performed?

✦What is your personal success rate for this procedure?

✦Will I need to undergo anesthesia during this procedure?

✦If so, what type of anesthesia will be required?

✦If so, have you and the anesthesiologist worked together before?

✦Will the procedure take place in a private hospital, outpatient
  clinic, or at the doctor's personal clinic?If at a private clinic, how
  nearby is an intensive care unit in case of emergency?

✦How often do you conduct procedures at that clinic or hospital?

✦What happens if something goes wrong and I need additional
  treatment or another operation?

✦Who will be required to pay for any additional fees?

✦How long will I be hospitalized?

✦How soon after the procedure can I fly?

✦What is not included in the price of the procedure?

✦Is there any insurance coverage for this procedure?

RETIRED LIFE

Live in a place where as your age increases so does your level of respect from the community

One size does not fit all, nor does one way of retiring fit every retired individual. This transition is not to be taken lightly. Just as your transition into adolescence, adulthood, and possibly parenthood were taken seriously so too should your transition into your wisest stage.

When considering a move to another country, you are in an ideal time to sit and reevaluate the person that you are today. Your life experiences have shaped you and groomed you to be who you are, don't base your decisions on the person you were in the 60s, 70s, or 80s. Instead, decide what is important to you now, and what you want to be important to you now? Reshape your life based on your answers. Moving abroad gives you a unique gift, a reset button to recreate yourself. Don't waste it.

In Thailand the country welcomes retirees and holds a great beautiful respect for elders. While North Americans often force retirement on their elders and send them into homes, Thailand holds utmost respect for those who have walked more steps on this earth. In addition to respect, the cost of living is as cheap as it gets and the weather is warm all year round.

Maybe it's been awhile since you really sat down and thought about what you want. Planning your retirement is a great time to stop and evaluate your life: what you enjoy, where you want to be, what's important to you, and what's holding you back?

PRIORITIES

Think about what's important to you. Something you want to cultivate? Is it family, health, hobbies, financial security, adventures, simplicity, or community? Write down the top 10 things that are most important to you. Structure your retirement around them. If you're hitched, have your spouse do the same and find a way to accomplish both of your needs and wants.

It's important to shape your retirement based on what you want, not what's really expected from you. How do you envision your golden years and how does Thailand fit into it? Do you see yourself as a part-time expat (see the next section) or a full time expat.

ACTIVITIES

Hobbies are important once you retire. Suddenly you have more time than you know what to do with. One of the biggest challenges with many transitioning into retirement is to avoid boredom. Thailand has countless activities that can help keep you mentally and physically fit:

✦ Settle in. Moving to Thailand will keep you busy for at least a year as you try new foods, explore the markets, make friends and try and understand why people are smiling at you
✦ Learn how to ride a motorbike
✦ Hiking and cycling around the city, taking sunset strolls at the beach, or take a dip in the ocean

- Join a sports team. Thailand has hundreds of different sports for all ages (thanks to the diverse expat population)
- Learn Thai (or Chinese, Japanese, Russian, French or Spanish). There are countless languages on offer to learn and a 30 hour course will cost as little as $100 if you don't require the accompanying *Education visa (the under 50's 'retirement' visa of choice)*
- Learn to cook Thai food. The street vendors make it look so easy but it's harder than you might realize and takes some practice. Ingredients for Thai food are super cheap
- Read or write. With lots of second hand book shops, you'll finally have the time to read the epic War and Peace, or write your own memoir
- Gardening. Unfortunately, allotments aren't common but most houses come with a large garden for you to work out that green thumb
- Join a community group or attend a quiz night. People take quizzes seriously down here. It's a real mental workout
- Travel. Once you have set yourself up in Thailand it is cheap to travel to neighboring countries and around South East Asia. Since you're not tied down to a job, you can travel during off season or ask for discounted weekday hotel rooms
- Work: just because you're retired doesn't mean you can't work if you want to. It just means work is on your terms now. Many retirees opt to teach English part-time, as a hobby and for extra spending money
- Start a business. Always wanted to set up your own restaurant or bar? Or you could sell your handy crafts on www.etsy.com

HEALTHY LIVING

Maintaining a healthy diet and lifestyle at any age is important. As with any country, you can live off a bad diet or a good one in Thailand. The big difference is that healthy living is incredibly cheap and accessible. In fact, a salad or vegetable stir fry is often cheaper than McDonalds. Fresh fruit smoothies and pre-prepared cut fruit is available outside every 7-Eleven. Thailand is home to hundreds of exotic fruits and vegetables and the traditional plant and rice based diet keeps Thais lean. There are also plenty of exercise options available from walking to gyms, health studios and yoga classes (there's a 60 year old retired woman in my yoga class that puts us all to shame). I often see retirees power walking in the early mornings (before the heat) and glowing with vitality – now that's the kind of retirement I want!

LOVE LIFE

It's easy to fall into complacency, aiming at just surviving in life. Make a focused effort to rid your complacent habits and thrive, not survive! Experience each moment and appreciate what life is offering you in the now. Fall into love with life again. Just as a relationship has to be watered time and time again to keep it fresh and alive, so too does your soul and outlook on life.

It's never too late for love either. Some retirees see Thailand as a place to start again with a Thai partner. Age differences don't really matter here as long as both partners are happy. Thais are much more easy going, friendly, and open to talk to. Expats living in Thailand moved here for similar reasons that you did so you'll already have a lot in common.

If you're married, exploring Thailand is even more fun. Thais love to see couples (they're big romantics) and will approach you to ask a load of questions. Relocating together can bring a second wind into a relationship. Gone are the roles, responsibilities, work, and compromises you've made for the other. Your fresh start with that person you fell in love with years ago awaits you in Thailand, the land of smiles. The most important thing about relocating together is communication. You'll both need to express your desires and fears and commit to support each other. What if one person doesn't like Thailand? You need to think and talk through various options so that you're prepared as a couple. Take your time, do things together but also separately to ensure a successful transition into expat life in Thailand.

MANAGE FEARS

Most Common Fears in Your Golden Years:

✦You will outlive your money
✦You will lose your marbles
✦You will spend your last years alone

Take action with something you are passionate about as a direct rebuttal to fear. Taking action is the opposite of being a victim. Outliving your money in Thailand is doubtful. Many expats opt to work part-time to keep their minds sharp and have extra spending money. Bangkok always ranks in top 10 surveys[67] for best quality of life, affordability and ease of living. Plan a budget, put some money aside for emergency flights home and stop worrying about the Benjamins - life's too short!

Many Americans fear that crime outside of the States is bad, or that the rest of the world hates Americans (I've met many Americans in the US who have this idea). It's totally the opposite. Crime in Thailand is incredibly low, with the exception of Bangkok's night scene, the worst crime you're likely to experience is paying *farang* price for a t-shirt (i.e. paying $4 more because they assume you can afford it).

While there is crime, it's the exception rather than the norm. I would argue that Thailand is safer than any city in the US. I always see petite bank clerks in heels filling up the ATMs and

---

[67] A Wall Street Journal article ranking Thailand number 1: http://bit.ly/thainumber1

think how in any other country, they use armored vehicles and bodyguards. Occasionally, there is petty theft e.g. by bye iPhone. The tourist police are really friendly, albeit useless, and will help you fill out insurance claim forms.

FAMILY & FRIENDS

Having a community of friends will greatly improve your expat experience. Expats in Thailand are very friendly and I guarantee after a week or two in Thailand, you'll have friends. At first your family might be upset you're moving half way around the world, after all, who will babysit for free on Saturday evening now? Sit them down and share with them what is important to you and why you want to move. Don't forget to mention that you will be an awesome tour-guide for them, and they now have a reason to take an amazing vacation to Thailand every year! See the *Family* section for lots of things to do with the grandchildren when they come to visit.

It's quite common to meet expats in their 30's and 40's who are retired. They've made and saved enough money to live comfortably here. It doesn't take as much money as you'd think to accomplish this. They have simplified, budgeted, and reduced their spending, paid off their debts, and don't want to work jobs they dislike just for the sake of money.

You can secure a retirement visa at 50 years old and need to show either $25,000 in a bank account or a monthly pension of $2,000. This gives you a one year non-immigrant O-A visa (long stay) that you can extend annually.

Recommended Books:

- *You Can Retire Sooner Than You Think* [68] by Wes Moss
- *Aging Bravely, Shut Up and Stop Your Whining* [69] by Dana Racinskas
- *How to Retire Happy, Wild, and Free: Retirement Wisdom That You Won't Get from Your Financial Advisor* [70] by Ernie Zelinski
- *65 things to Do When You Retire* [71]
- *The Couples Retirement Puzzle: 10 Must-Have Conversations for Transitioning to the Second Half of Life* [72] Robert Taylor and Dorian Mintzer

---

[68] http://bit.ly/retiresoonermoss

[69] http://bit.ly/agingbravely

[70] http://bit.ly/retirewild

[71] http://bit.ly/65tdretire

[72] http://bit.ly/coupleconversations

THE PART-TIME EXPAT "SNOW BIRDER"

Moving full-time is just not in the cards for some folks, be it receiving their GSI (Canadians), wanting to see their grand babies more frequently, or just because you might want both lives (the one you've cultivated for the last many years and the life you have part-time in Thailand). If you are not confident to jump into the deep-end, why not dip your feet in?

Quit your job, sell your home, say goodbye to your family and friends and pack up, ship and relocate your whole life. It's a bit daunting. If you know Thailand is where you want to be – great. If you can't imagine missing a birthday or Christmas with your family then maybe consider a middle ground – living in Thailand part-time.

Everybody has an ideal balance of home and away. For me 'away' suits me very well but for others you might miss your community and feel that 'home' is equally important. How about only spending 3 or 6 months in Thailand? Dividing your time might even mean win-win! Trade the harsh winters for cool sea breezes, Thailand's hot season for a real spring and summer at home! While not everyone divides their time between here and home, a fair few expats do. Consider the cost of flights, transfers and distance when deciding your time divide.

$$ LIFESTYLE

Can you afford the lifestyle you desire where you currently live on your retirement budget? If the answer is no, then ask yourself if you lived in Thailand half of the year with more luxuries for less money, would that help you fill the gap in your lifestyle goals? Make sure and consider/budget flight expenses and travel insurance.

Do you strive for continuity? For your six months abroad, will you want to return to Thailand each time or do you think you'll want the freedom to explore other affordable countries in the years to come? Say Ecuador, Malaysia, or Mexico?

THE BALANCING ACT

Living in more than one location is inherently more work. There are double the utilities to turn on, off, and manage. If you rent out one or both of your homes, you add an additional depth of complexity. Decorating, stocking, and maintaining homes in two countries can prove exhausting. In the end, most things worth doing are difficult. Living outside the box, in two boxes rather, may be the best arrangement for you and yours. Organization and planning are key components to help tame the additional responsibilities.

Good friends of mine, Lisa and Junior, have the goal of living a third of the year across three properties: their lake house in Virginia, their beach front estate in Roatan, and are currently looking for their third spot. They plan to rent each property while they are away, creating a passive income while living their dream. They have it all figured out!

PROPERTY MANAGEMENT

If you opt to buy property in Thailand that you only occupy part-time you can rent the property when you're not there. You could also have a neighbor keep an eye on your house for you, hire a house-sitter, or even make a house-swap and live in a new country rent-free.

TRAVEL INSURANCE

If you plan on spending less than a year in Thailand, it's worth purchasing travel insurance to cover any medical emergencies you may have. Make sure your plan covers medical evacuation. Travel insurance can cover emergency hospital visits, expenses accrued by flight delays, and luggage replacement. See *Healthcare* section for more information about what's available.

EXPAT EXPERIENCE

"I've been coming here on and off for about 32 years. Now I work offshore as a metallurgist (chemical engineer) and commute every 2 weeks to Australia. I guess because I don't maintain any residence in Australia, I'm really a Thai resident....

Coming and going is very easy and compared to last decade, it's even cheaper. My type of work requires constant travel. A lot of my peers live on the east side of Australia. I not only pay less for airfare, in most cases I'm actually home before they are! With my work roster, I rarely need to worry about visas since I'm granted the standard 30 days on arrival with no paperwork or hassle. I'm legally married here and having children, so I'm eligible for several types of visas, but I really don't see the point until I get closer to retirement.

I have consciously chosen to raise my family here. I believe the culture and education system here is better for them. I have 11 year old twin girls who are my top priority. Also, the lifestyle that my income can sustain is far better here compared to either of my 2 "home" countries (I'm English born with Australian citizenship). Lastly, I find it safer and the people friendlier than in either of those two countries."

~ Chris Taylor, Australian/British, Engineer

THE MOVING BLUES

No country is 100% perfect, although some beaches in southern Thailand come close! Moving to Thailand won't solve all your problems, make you happier, or fix your relationship. I'm sad to say that any emotional baggage you have will be shipped with you to your new home. However, Thailand is the land of smiles and it's a great environment to heal, grow, and live in.

In every move I've made, I've experienced a roller coaster of emotions. If you plan for it, it can take the edge off a little. Expect to have an initial high followed by an intense low. The low is mostly due to loneliness, culture shock which will be discussed next, and inaccurate expectations.

Change causes stress no matter what kind of stress it is. Moving to an amazing country that fits you perfectly is still a stressful event. There are concerns you will have and worries of endless logistics: shipping your luggage, pets, new house, new area, language acquisition, new foods, access to utilities, etc.

A key method for quick acclimation is to go out and make friends in the community. Find out the inner workings of the community and how you can contribute. If you spend all day interacting with those you left back home on Skype or magicJack then you've only left in body and are cheating your experience.

Thai people will guide you to appreciate every moment and point out the beauty in everything. The cost of living is lower so suddenly you don't need to worry about money, and you will probably lose weight due to all the delicious healthy foods available. It's a great thing when Taco Bell and McDonalds aren't the cheapest and most easily accessible food any longer.

You'll have more time to examine your life and make the changes to become the person you've always known you were. Thailand also offers every opportunity to distract yourself, however, with time your old problems will re-emerge, and you'll feel restless – hello moving blues.

CULTURE SHOCK

Everyone has heard of culture shock. You've seen it time and again on TV when the host is guiding you through Chinas markets or a journalist is exploring India. They have a disorientated look about them. Merriam -Webster describes it as *"A sense of confusion and uncertainty sometimes with feelings of anxiety that may affect people exposed to an alien culture or environment without adequate preparation."* However, even with preparation you're gonna feel it.

There are four stages to culture shock and it's important to identify where you are and why you're feeling this way.

THE HONEYMOON STAGE

This is a euphoric narcotic-free (we hope) high. Everything you see is new and amazing: the people, the attitude, the lifestyle, and the food. You see no wrong in the country and wonder why you didn't move here sooner. You imagine you'll be here for the rest of your life and, just like a new relationship, you're blind to any faults your partner may have. After the initial high, you come falling back onto the asphalt. Small things start to nag at you: when your food comes too spicy to eat, when the same taxi driver offers you outrageous *farang* prices everyday, careless driving and people's inability to understand what you are saying in Thai because you're using the wrong tone, the street dogs incessant barking, and the foul sewer oders. Errrrrr.....

NEGOTIATION STAGE

This is when reality settles in. When you sit down and wonder what have you done? All of the differences initially seen as romantic are all of the sudden cause for great concern. Can you really do this? Can you adjust to so many differences?

You realize how incredibly far away you are from "home" and your family. Maybe you don't know a soul in Thailand. While many Thai speak English, there is still a language barrier keeping you from fully integrating. While you can't see the barrier, you feel it in every interaction. You feel it when you have trouble ordering meat at the butcher counter, paying your water bill, finding the sugar in the supermarket, or asking the bus driver how much is the fare. Additionally, it's hard to adjust to the tropical climate (beach goers) and new food.

This phase is not pleasant and those who successfully navigate through it are gentle and patient with themselves. They also laugh at their mistakes, learn from others, and resolve that they are no longer in a hurry and no longer in the US. They learn and adopt realistic expectations.

ADJUSTMENT STAGE

By now you have shifted your expectations, become accustomed to the differences and the little things no longer bother you. Bad drivers – not your problem, people don't understand your Thai – speak English. You've adopted the *Mai Pen Rai* ('it doesn't matter') attitude of Thailand. From this point, you will start to unravel a deeper level of Thai culture.

TIP
Thais love to have fun and be in the moment. As with many tropical countries, they don't worry about tomorrow because there's always food growing on the trees. Lack of planning is a common complaint amongst expats, but it's part of Thailand's charm and hospitality.

MASTERY STAGE

You are 100% comfortable in your new life. You accept the cultural differences and often participate in Thai cultural events. You won't lose your old self but are now an expert in the Thai way. You understand the differences, know how to tackle them, and are ready and able to help mentor a new expat.

Finally, don't forget you're in Thailand! Every time I feel a little burned out with expat life, I call a friend back home who tells me I'm not missing anything and that I'm crazy to be homesick! She always puts things in perspective.

★   *If you felt this book helped you in your decision and / or preparation for the move to Thailand please consider reviewing it on Amazon. Thank you, and enjoy your journey.*

BASIC PHRASES TO GET YOU STARTED

Thai has different endings for male or female speakers
polite endings for male – *kup*
polite endings for female – *ka*
e.g. Hello (m) *Sa-wa-dee kup*
Thai also has different 'I' for male and females – *I (m) pom. I (f) chan*

Hello	*Sa-wa-dee ka/kup (f/m)*
How are you?	*Sabai - dee mai*
I'm fine	*Sabai-dee*
I'm not well	*(m/f) pom/chan mai - sabai*

Thank you	*kup-koon - ka/kup (f/m)*
Please	*Ga-ruu-na*
You are welcome / It doesn't matter	*mai -bpen - rai*
Goodbye	*sa-wa-dee ka/kup (f/m)*
Yes	*Chai*
No	*Mai Chai*

Language   *pa-sa*
Thai language   *pa-sa Thai*
English language   *pa-sa angrit*
Do you speak English?   *poot pa-sa angrit dai mai*
I don't speak Thai   *poot pa-sa Thai mai dai*
I don't understand   *mai kao jai*
I understand   *kao jai*
I'm sorry   *kor-tod   ka/kup   (f/m)*
Where is the bathroom?   *Hong-nam tee nai*

My name is ....   *(m/f) pom/chan cheu ..*
I am an American   *(m/f) pom/chan bpen khon Ah-mer-e-gan*
I am Canadian   *(m/f) pom/chan bpen khon ka-naa-daa*
I am British   *(m/f) pom/chan bpen khon Angrit*

Boy   *puu chai*
Girl   *puu ying*

I like ....   *(m/f) pom/chan chop....*

Eat   *gin*
Drink   *doom*
Fruit   *pol-la-mai*
Restaurant   *arhan*
Can I have....   *kor...*
Rice   *kao*
Chicken fried rice   *kao pad gai*
Spicy   *pet*
Is this spicy?   *An-nee pet mai*
I don't want it spicy   *mai pet*

Check/ bill please   *gep tang / check -bin*

Good   *dee*
Bad   *mai dee*

How much is this?   *An-nee tow rai*
It's cheap   *tuk mak*
It's expensive   *peng mak*
Can you give me a discount? *Lot-noi dai mai*
I'll take it   *aow*

1   *nung*
2 *song*
3 *saam*
4 *see*
5 *haa*
6 *hok*
7 *jet*
8 *bet*
9 *gao*
10 *sip*
20 *yee sip*
30 *saam sip*
40 *see sip*
50 *haa sip*
100   *nung roy*
500 *haa roy*
1,000   *nung paan*

COOL STUFF/ RESOURCES

Helpful resources to jumpstart your Thai life

ACTIVITIES

Meet some elephants www.elephantnaturepark.org

10 day silent meditation course
www.suanmokkh-idh.org/idh-travel.html

Take a massage course at ITM school
www.itmthaimassage.com

Motorbike touring www.gt-rider.com and
www.diymotorcycletours.net.au

Luxury boats and private
charters. www.thaiislandcruising.com

BLOGS

The ultimate Thailand Blogger www.richardbarrow.com

A list of Thai blogs www.hailandbloggers.com
Cafe review in Chiang Mai
www.chiangmaicoffeeculture.com
Thaizer Blog: www.thaizer.com

FOOD

The 10 best dishes
www.phuket.com/cuisine/toptenfood.htm

HOTELS

Website with great hotel discounts www.agoda.com
Budget hostel chain in Bkk www.lubd.com
An eco resort near Chiang Mai chailaiorchid.com
Thai hotel chain www.centarahotelsresorts.com

JOB LISTINGS

For teachers
www.ajarn.com/recruitment/browse_jobs/index.html
For careers www.careerjet.co.th

IMMIGRATION

Thai embassy Washington DC www.thaiembdc.org/dcdp
Thailand's visa information
www.thaiembassyuk.org.uk/?q=node/4

LEGAL
www.siam-legal.com
www.sunbeltlegaladvisors.com

A good list of lawyers www.thailawforum.com/lawyer.html

NEWS
www.bangkokpost.com
www.nationmultimedia.com/index.php

PROPERTY MANAGEMENT
Samui property www.overseaspropertyportfolio.com
Bangkok property www.property-bangkok.com and
www.siampropertygroup.com

ONLINE GROUPS
Facebook – Desperately seeking Bangkok
Facebook - Phuket New Era Expats
Facebook - Community Online Pin Board Koh Samui
Facebook – what's happening in Chiang Mai
Facebook - Koh Phangan Conscious Community

ONLINE FORUMS
Everything you need to know www.thaivisa.com/forum

SERVICES
Online dating site www.thaifriendly.com

SCHOOLS
International school listing http://www.isat.or.th/index.php
Learn Thai www.thaiwalen.com
TEFL training centre www.samuitefl.com

THAI LANGUAGE
Online dictionary www.Thai2English.com
Learn Thai www.thaiwalen.com

Learn Thai from A white Guy:
learnthaifromawhiteguy.com